Presents

Discovering the Mind of a Woman

Unless otherwise indicated, Scripture references are taken from the King James version of the Bible. Other versions which are used by permission are:

THE AMPLIFIED VERSION OF THE OLD TESTAMENT, Copyright © 1962, 1964 by The Zondervan Publishing House. Used by permission.

THE NEW AMERICAN STANDARD BIBLE Copyright © The Lockman Foundation, 1969, 1962, 1963, 1968, 1971, 1972, 1973, 1975, and 1977. Used by permission.

THE AMPLIFIED VERSION OF THE NEW TESTAMENT Copyright © The Lockman Foundation, 1954, 1958. Used by permission.

THE HOLY BIBLE, NEW INTERNATIONAL VERSION Copyright © 1978 by New York International Bible Society. Used by permission.

Discovering the Mind of a Woman
© Copyright 1982
By Ken Nair
Third Printing June 1986
ISBN #0-937929-00-X

This is written, particularly, with the Christian in mind. Because of that, there are some definitions that need to be made for those who are reading this and may not be Christians.

THE SPIRIT . . . . The inner person, in contrast to the physical body. (Romans 3:16)
The heart of a being.
The center; where character is developed.
The conscience.

WOUNDING
THE SPIRIT . . . . Attacking the character of another person.
Causing others to feel rejected.

DIE TO SELF . . . . Setting aside self interests.
Putting God and His ways above self. Acknowledging the difference between Christ and self and making the necessary changes.

SPIRITUAL LEADERSHIP . . . . One who is learning and is applying God's ways.
Becoming an example that others can follow.

HUMAN GLORY . . . . Godliness in a person that can be seen by others.

HEALING OTHERS
EMOTIONALLY . . . . Causing a person who feels emotionally, spiritually and/or physically worthless, to feel through my attitudes, actions and words toward them, that they are very valuable and acceptable; helping them to feel the love of God through me; changing their discouraged, hurting, purposeless lives into encouraged, helpful, purposeful lives.

TABLE OF CONTENTS

Dedicated to the glory of God with gratefulness for His perfect plan which included for me a helpmeet who has shown such unbelievable love and patience while I struggled and continue to struggle with learning to be the husband she deserves.

I love you Nancy.

CHAPTER ONE

DISCOVERING THREE KEYS FOR A SUCCESSFUL MARRIAGE

> Do you know that a man can learn how to understand the mind of a woman? He may, however, have to change the desires of his heart.

Understanding the mind of a woman is really not so difficult. There is no great puzzle or mystery to unravel. But to learn of it does require that a man make a serious commitment.

There are three major concepts to be understood in this chapter. If these concepts become the desires of a man's heart, they will develop a marriage relationship that will match or exceed his highest expectations. Unfortunately, too often a man is unwilling to consider his responsibility before God to understand his wife. A man should know, however, that a genuinely successful marriage cannot be had without the oneness that comes from a man and wife knowing each other's innermost secret selves.

The purpose of this book is to help every man see the need to illustrate Christ to his wife, which includes knowing the heart of his wife and understanding her innermost feelings. Included in this aim is also the intent to show how the Lord makes it possible for a man to learn these things. It is remarkable to see how much, as a man endeavors to gain understanding from the Lord's own examples, he will develop the ability to understand the mind of a woman.

PREPARATION FOR DISCOVERING THE CONCEPTS

My marriage was not one that was marked by gross immorality or by severe physical or mental abuse. It was, instead, quite normal. I suppose there were even those who thought we had a marriage that could be used as an example. I do know that I really thought I was an excellent example of a good husband. But while working hard at doing all the things I believed would build my marriage, I was actually tearing it apart, destroying it.

During the first ten years of our marriage, the Lord knew I didn't have the kind of marriage He wanted me to have. He also knew that it would never be possible for me to have the kind of marriage He wanted unless some changes were made in my life. These changes were not likely to take place, however, unless I could first gain an understanding of **three major concepts** that are absolutely vital for a successful marriage. He knew, too, that I had **no** idea that these three major concepts even existed, so He proceeded to set up the circumstances that would reveal them to me.

Here's how God worked it out:

Because they saw that my dedication to their ministry was unlimited, a nationally-known Christian organization invited me in

December 1970, to join their staff. This was quite an enviable opportunity. Many people have dreamed about working for this organization. My wife and I were both very excited about this special privilege that we felt God was giving us. We packed our household furnishings into the moving van, and we were free to leave for our destination. We made the trip from California to Chicago in a plane, so naturally, we arrived sooner than our furniture did. As a matter of fact, it turned out that we arrived several weeks before our furniture was to arrive. This was, of course, not a coincidence. God's plan was to use our tardy furniture to bring into sharp focus a lesson that He was preparing for me.

We had been in our barren house for three weeks when an announcement was made that the staff of the organization of which I was now a member would be going on a staff retreat lasting for several days. It would also be several hundred miles away. Now, as it happened, the same day this announcement was made my wife and I received word that our furniture would arrive on the same day the staff was to leave for the retreat. My wife was not only unaccustomed to the idea of her husband being gone from home, but she was not at all excited about being the one to oversee the task of unloading a truck full of furniture. Nor was she thrilled about trying to get the house organized with two young children underfoot and no husband to help. This was in the middle of winter with snow and slush everywhere. Can you guess how she reacted to this news? You're right; she became very discouraged and upset, even angry.

"Oh no!" I thought. "How can my wife embarrass me like this? She's going to ruin my reputation as a husband who has everything and everyone in his family 'in line'. She's going to make me look bad in the eyes of my new boss. Is she going to ruin my chances of being with the staff on this special outing? Is she going to destroy my chances to be part of this great ministry? What shall I do?"

I tried explaining to her how I had no choice in the matter. After all, it was a standard policy and practice there to have retreats. It was part of the job. Nothing soothed her disposition. Finally it occurred to me: I would ask her to talk to the boss! That was it!

What a stroke of genius! Let him explain to her how unreasonable she was being. She wouldn't dare dispute **his** words about her attitudes!

While I was at work that Friday afternoon, my wife and my boss talked on the phone. I felt confident that everything was going to work out just fine. She would be able to see how she needed to re-evaluate her unrealistic thinking. Imagine, her demanding that I stay home while all the other staff went away!

Although the conversation between them was completed several hours before the work day was done, I had not heard from my boss. As I was getting ready to walk home, the boss told me that I would not be going with them to the retreat. Although outwardly I may have seemed willing to accept what my boss had said, inwardly I was boiling about this decision because I knew what motivated it.

THE IMPORTANT CONCEPTS REVEALED

Walking home, I became even more angry. When I was about thirty yards from home, the Holy Spirit impressed upon my mind some very startling thoughts.

I was thinking, "How could she do this to me? She's ruined me. Now I'll never be able to work in a meaningful way in this ministry." My bitterness was increasing by the minute. Then the Holy Spirit helped me realize that the bitterness and resentment within me were there because I was going to have to stay home with my family instead of getting to be with others who were practically strangers to me. I was even more disturbed when I realized that those were exactly the opposite of what my thoughts should have been. They were also the exact opposite of the very design of the ministry that I had joined: a ministry to build families.

I realized then that I did not really desire to put my family first. I was not seeking to meet my wife's needs. I didn't even know how! I didn't know how to genuinely love my wife or anyone else for that matter. How could I be the spiritual leader of my home especially if I weren't sensitive to the idea of others having a Spirit? I began to wonder, "What really is a spiritual leader?"

Have you ever been confronted with these thoughts?

Just as the apostle Peter (John 21:17) had to be confronted with his inadequacies before he could receive from God the understanding that would make him more adequate, so too, I had to become aware of my miserable condition before I could: 1. plead for God's mercy and instructions, and 2. ask that He open the doorway to greater understanding.

THE THREE CONCEPTS

Confronted with my miserable condition, I found myself pleading with God for these three things:

1. That God would help me learn how to meet the needs of my wife, to understand her mind, her way of thinking, her innermost feelings.

2. That God would show me how to love my wife so that she would be able to experience more than just hearing me say, "I love you." As God's representative, I wanted her to experience God loving her through me! This would include learning how to love her from her frame of reference. I wanted God to bless her heart through me.

3. That I could learn how to be the spiritual leader of my home and that my spirit might become so sensitive that I would become aware of the Holy Spirit actually leading my spirit.

I had no idea at that time what asking God for these three teachings would require of me. Had I known ahead of time. I might not have made these three requests. But now, having gone through testings and sufferings and having experienced blessings and benefits, I have assurance that we can never pay more than God gives in return for yielding to His ways.

"For it became him, for whom are all things, and by whom are all things, in bringing many sons unto Glory to make the captain of their salvation perfect through suffering." (Hebrews 2:10)

If we expect to become Christ-like, should we be any less willing to experience suffering than Christ was? (I Peter 2:24)

CHAPTER TWO

GETTING
DOWN TO BUSINESS

It's easy to say, "I want God's will." But, do you really want to be the husband that God wants you to be?

ELIMINATING REACTIONS

I once watched a friend do something that changed the pattern of my life. We were managing a week-long convention that could only accommodate 3,500 people. Months earlier it had already reached the attendance capacity through pre-registration. However, on the first night of the convention there were some people who came hoping they could still register. But because it was already full, they were told that if they wished, they could wait until the conference began. If there were any cancellations, they would be able to attend.

Imagine the anticipation as 200 people waited nearly three hours to see if there would be any vacancies. Each person was relating to us and to each other his reasons for believing that he should get in. Finally the convention began, and my friend, who was also my superior, said to me, "We have enough room to let these people in." I was very excited for them all. "Great," I said, "let me go tell them!"

I wanted to go over to where they were waiting, get their attention and exclaim, "I've got good news for you, you can all get in!" But my friend said, "No, I'll take care of it." I will never forget seeing him do something that since then has saved me countless problems.

He got their attention by saying, "We have good news and bad news. First the good news. It seems as though there is enough room for you to get in tonight." After much excited commotion on the part of the group, he added these very important words: "Now the bad news. You probably will have to stand all evening (three hours), which means you will be in the back of the auditorium where it will be difficult to see and hear. Then, too, if the people who had already registered before you show up tomorrow night, you won't be able to get in for the rest of the week. With this in mind, do you still want to attend?"

Of course, every one of them did. The benefit of his handling the situation in this manner was that not one of them would be able to legitimately complain at the end of the session saying they were uncomfortable and couldn't hear or see well. Nor could they say that they were not made aware of the unfavorable conditions. This would free them to benefit from the convention, because they would not be distracted by resentments.

I think the contents of this book need the same treatment. There needs to be some mental preparation for the difficulties that lie ahead. I won't blame you if what this book says makes you want to throw it down and jump up and down on it; nor if you get mad at me. But please don't throw it down without first giving it careful consideration.

I recall a section of scripture about a man who wanted to share in the glory of Christ's ministry and asked Jesus what was involved in becoming a partner. Jesus warned him that it was, from a human standpoint, very undesirable to follow Him. (Matthew 8:20) The same thing is true of the principles this book presents. From a human standpoint, they appear very undesirable, but they bring rich rewards.

WHAT IS THE FIRST STEP?

Purge yourself!

"Search me, O God, and know my heart: try me, and know my thoughts: and see if there be any wicked way in me, and lead me in the way everlasting." (Psalm 139: 23, 24)

Are you ready to permit God to search you and try you in this way? This verse is extremely demanding. While there may be many of us men who can recite this verse, it seems as though many of us are unwilling to apply it to ourselves, especially in our marriages.

It is the God Who loves us and wants His best for us and Who is bringing reproofs into our lives. He wants all Christians to be purged of their un-Christ-like ways.

It is very natural to get angry and to defend ourselves. It is especially hard to resist those natural inclinations of anger and self-defense when God has designed a trial to draw our attention to our failures or our inadequacies. It must grieve God's heart to see how so few of us who claim Christianity behave in a Christ-like manner when in the midst of a trial. God really does want those of us who are His to be perfected.

"I know, O Lord, that thy judgments are right and that thou in faithfulness hast afflicted me." (Psalm 119:75)

"The ear that heareth the reproof of life abideth among the wise. He that refuseth instruction despiseth

his own soul: but he that heareth reproof getteth under-
standing." (Proverbs 15:31, 32)
Even though it's not always enjoyable, I must let God purge me. I
fear the loss of my closeness to God, if I do not.

This book is written with a special purpose in mind. It is not
written for women. There are already many books for women.
Rather, this book is written entirely for men. Its intention is to draw
attention specifically to the inadequate thinking and attitudes that
prevent men from enjoying the special joys and benefits that come
from learning to understand the mind of a woman.

Further, the purpose of this book is to develop in men more
Christ-like attitudes and responses as they learn to live with their
wives in an understanding way. (I Peter 3:7) This book is intended
to convey an entirely different perspective from what might com-
monly be conveyed about the responsibilities we husbands have
to our wives. It is not the desire here to put blame on men or to
point an accusing finger at men, but rather, to illustrate problems
between husbands and wives and then to show how to change
some of the thinking that may actually be blocking the solutions to
those problems.

As this progresses, men are going to be asked to reconsider
some traditional thinking. I know how threatening it can be to have
our traditional "Christian" ways and thought patterns challenged,
especially if we've been living with them for years and they have
been accepted as normal. But we do have an obligation as Christians to challenge all things in the light of this truth; even though
they may be traditionally accepted, are my ways actually examples
of Christ-likeness?

*"Despise not prophesyings. **Prove all things; hold fast***
that which is good." *(I Thessalonians 5:20, 21)*
One particular challenge will involve asking men to give up their
marriage "thrones" and to stop thinking of themselves as the boss,
king, emperor or possibly even the dictator. An aspect of that will
include asking men to consider the need for men to earn positions
of leadership by dying to self (putting self last, preferring wife and
others first). This does not mean ignoring our responsibilities as
husbands; it means re-evaluating our attitudes.

We need to prove ourselves as leaders through examples of humility and serving others and to create in our wives and others a desire to follow us.

Consider Philippians 2:5-9:

"Let this mind be in you, which was also in Christ Jesus: Who, being in the form of God, (did not regard equality with God a thing to be grasped.) But made himself of no reputation, and took upon him the form of a servant, and was made in the likeness of men; and being found in fashion as a man, He humbled himself, and became obedient unto death, even the death of the cross. Wherefore God also hath highly exalted him, and given Him a name which is above every name." (K.J.V. & N.A.S.B.)

When confronted with the thought of giving up his "throne", a man will sometimes ask some of these rather natural questions:

"Is that wise?"

"Can a man's kingdom function if he steps down from being the king?"

"Is focusing almost exclusively on myself first a necessary aspect of seeking the kingdom of God and His righteousness?"

"Is it safe? Who will protect my kingdom?" Ought not a man have the confidence that our loving heavenly Father will be quick to protect this man's kingdom...especially if He knows that this man has made a commitment to become Christ-like, purposing to learn how to yield his throne to Christ. Then, in turn, a man needs to learn he can only rightfully occupy the throne he thought was his by becoming Christ's representative on that throne.

God's will is that every man first remove the beam from his own eye (purging himself first). God prefers that a man learn to lead others through the instructions of Christ-like examples, rather than by attempting to instruct with words only.

"But be ye doers of the word, and not hearers only, deceiving your own selves. For if any be hearer of the word, and not a doer, he is like unto a man beholding his natural face in a glass: For he beholdeth himself, and goeth his way, and straightway forgetteth what manner of man he was. But whoso looketh into the perfect law of liberty, and continueth therein, he being not a

forgetful hearer, but **a doer of the word,** *this man shall
be blessed in his deed."* (James 1:22, 25)

Contrary to popular notions, most wives do not want to occupy
the throne in their marriages. A wife wants her husband to be her
leader, but she feels especially secure when she sees that her
husband is not the final authority in their marriage, that he is looking
to God for direction and guidance. Then she knows that their
relationship will be based on scriptural principles and not on her
husband's personal preferences which she recognizes can be very
prejudiced or selfishly motivated. When a husband discovers that
his wife feels that he is prejudiced or selfish, rather than argue with
her, he should be willing to learn what he can do to restore her
confidence in him.

A husband should know that in the eyes of God, becoming
Christ-like is more important than is developing a "home govern-
ment" where the husband is established as King.

*"Mercy and truth preserve the King: and his throne is
upholden by mercy."* (Proverbs 20:28)

Worthy character traits for a leader definitely are mercy and
truth.

God is calling husbands to a new, deeper commitment to Himself. We need to continually examine more closely the differences
between ourselves and Christ and to determine that we will not
allow ourselves the freedom of making any excuse for the sin that
is revealed in our lives. (James 4:17)

Maybe, while reading, you may see the need to completely re-
evaluate some long standing notions. Perhaps you will be challenged in ways you have never been challenged before. Perhaps
you will find that what many are calling "a normal marriage" is not
what God calls "normal." Possibly then you will see the need to
exchange what you may have accepted as the "normal Christian
lifestyle" to a lifestyle that will be more demanding of you. Maybe
your utmost efforts will be required, especially in reference to
denial of self. Making a commitment to not assert yourself requires
focusing on developing self-control.

*"Then said Jesus unto his disciples, If any man will
come after me,* **let him deny himself,** *and take up his
cross and follow me."* (Matthew 16:24)

Becoming an example of Christ to one's wife is very demanding. It is, therefore, only fair to ask, "Are you ready for the kind of struggle this concept represents?" Because it will be a struggle!

> There is no other alternative but to commit to God the message contained in these pages, and ask that He will make clear and applicable its contents.

CHAPTER THREE

THREE
BASIC PROBLEMS

There are three prejudices about women that cloud the minds of most men. Could these prejudices be preventing men from understanding the mind of a woman?

I've found that in order for any problem to be solved, it must be approached directly and be examined very closely. But maybe you are like I am. Sometimes I ask questions, but I don't want to accept the answers if I don't like them. However, since it is my responsibility to solve problems in my marriage, finding only answers that I like, should not be my goal.

Self-examination is a form of problem solving. In order to deal with problems in our own lives, we must approach them directly and examine them closely. The idea of opening self up for examination makes some people so nervous that, when others are engaged in self-examination, they may try to stop them, insisting that they are being too self-critical or too introspective. Often I see people trying to eliminate self-examination from the Christian walk and I wonder if they fear that self-examination will result in limited freedoms for themselves. It would appear they are fearful of losing the freedom to do whatever they want and still profess to be leading Christian lives.

Sometimes people do not wish to engage in self-examination. They do not even want others to engage in self-examination, since there is an inner realization that if any one person, out of a desire to be more Christ-like, corrects his behavior, pressures come to bear on those around him who are not willing to change. Anyone who is becoming more Christ-like will stand out from that which is worldly.

If a businessman were to continually double check himself in his business, he would be considered a very thorough businessman. God wants us to be thorough in all that we do for Him too, even in our self-examination. *"For if we would judge ourselves, we should not be judged."* (I Corinthians 11:31)

Perhaps a word picture from Scripture will help illustrate the basic problems. In the Amplified Version Of The Bible, Psalm 51, verse 5 says:

> *"Behold, I was brought forth in a state of iniquity; my mother was sinful who conceived me and I, too, am sinful."*

And then, in Ephesians 6, verse 12, it says,

> *"For we are not wrestling with flesh and blood contending only with physical opponents — but against the despotisms, against the powers, against the master spirits who are the world rulers of this present darkness, against*

*the **spirit forces of wickedness** in the heavenly, supernatural, sphere."*

The following is my understanding of those two verses. Although this illustration will not be entirely accurate in its sequence, this is what I visualize. I see a baby being born, and there has been waiting impatiently, an evil presence which is, if you were able to see it, in the process of uniting itself with this new born baby. This evil presence has the power to become the controlling influence in this new life. This evil influence in mankind I call the "sin nature" or "lower nature". While the child is growing up with this evil inside himself, the child is not aware of its influence on his life or that its presence is undesirable and harmful to him. In fact, since this has happened to everyone, the child doesn't see himself as being different from anyone else. He may think about God, but he doesn't even consider that he is not the person God wants him to be, free from the control of evil. Nor does he consider that his life should be, instead, led by the Holy Spirit.

This evil spirit has joined each person, because he wants each person to be with him in hell. Therefore, God sent His Son, Jesus Christ, to make it possible for us to be saved from going to hell. We are saved by agreeing with God that we have this sin nature and that we have sinned and are in need of forgiveness and that Christ died for our sins and that God raised him from the dead. We need to believe and trust Him with the balance of our lives.

Then, believing that Christ is the Son of God and accepting Him as Savior, we are saved from hell. Next, we need to let the Holy Spirit be the influence in our lives. But evil still wants to control us, so the next goal of evil, after being forced out of us by God's Spirit, is to influence us even after we allow Jesus to become our Savior.

*"For I know that in me (that is, in my flesh,) dwelleth no good thing: for to will is present with me; but how to perform that which is good I find not. For the good that I would, I do not: but the evil which I would not, that I do. Now if I do that I would not, it is no more I that do it, **but sin that dwelleth in me.** I find then a law, that, when I would do good, **evil is present** with me. For I delight in the law of God after the inward man: But I see another law in my members, warring against the law of my mind, and bringing me into captivity to the law of sin which is in my members. O wretched man that I am! who shall*

*deliver me from the body of this death? I thank God
through Jesus Christ our Lord. So then with the mind I
myself serve the law of God; but with the flesh the law of
sin." (Romans 7:18-25)*

Evil does not want anyone to see his desperate need to invite
Jesus to become his Savior. Evil wants others to see no changes, no
joy, no purpose in being a Christian. That's why now that we are
Christians, we must **look at** and **examine** the contrasts between
Christ and ourselves, making the changes that will **show** others
what happens when Christ is not only our Savior, but our Lord as
well.

Remember, since the influence of evil in our lives is **not** something we can see (that is, not as we can see another person) we
don't easily recognize evil's influences. Then too, because this evil
(or sin-nature) is common to all of us, and isn't noticeable as would
be a grapefruit in a pile of apples, we don't even suspect that it is
with us. Therefore, we don't put ourselves on guard against it.

To **prevent** the spirit of evil from convincing others that
accepting Christ as Savior makes no difference, we must have a
willingness to examine our lives closely in the light of Christ and that
which leads to Christ-like living. Becoming Christ-like requires that
we let the Holy Spirit be our boss. This will result in a fulfilled,
meaningful life, benefitting not only ourselves but also those
around us. But, in contrast, a life led by the spirit of sin will result in a
frustrating meaningless life, full of destruction. The spirit of evil in
us, called ''sin nature'', is our enemy and the enemy of God, and
any enemy of God should be fought and defeated.

With the purpose in mind of examining self, here are three
problem areas to examine.

1. A MYSTERIOUS SUBJECT

As difficult as it is to get any two men to agree on any one
subject, there is, however, one subject on which you can get
almost all men to agree. In fact, because men are in such agreement on this subject, it is probably the most common source of
jokes and laughter among men. You can find out just how united
men are about this subject by asking them one simple question:
"Do you understand the way a woman thinks?"

''Nobody understands the way a woman thinks, not even
women,'' is the answer men will almost unanimously give, with an
air of superiority that is revealed by a laugh or smirk.

I remember hearing when I was a boy, about the impossibilities involved in figuring out women. As I grew up, I became even more aware that many men had accepted as a fact that the most certain thing about a woman's mind is that it is "fickle." What a shame! Because of the acceptance of this type of thinking, multiplied thousands of families are suffering needlessly.

Deep scars are being left in the hearts of some precious people, people who should be enjoying very special husband-wife relationships. Marriage relationships should be filled with love and understanding. God wants to use marriage as an illustration of how much He loves and understands His own.

I know how harmful it is to believe, "Women are impossible to understand," because that's what I once believed. I now recognize the scars that type of thinking can produce. I saw it scar my own marriage.

Can it be true that it is impossible for a man to understand the mind of a woman?

It is definitely not true!

God says in I Peter 3:7, *"Live with your wife in an understanding way."* But, most men will quickly admit that they don't know how to do this. Does it seem likely that God would really command us to do the impossible? Certainly not!

While it is true that there is a basic difference in the way men and women think,* the only difficulty in learning to understand that difference is in the heart of a man. Is he willing — or unwilling—to be a learner.

Why is the burden to develop understanding put on the man's shoulders? Because God wants it that way! The very essence of a spiritual leader is to assume full responsibility for leading.

I would love to see this book accomplish two goals:

1. To help man understand the ways a woman thinks, thereby removing from the minds of man and woman the stigma that the thinking that occurs in the mind of a woman is the opposite of good thinking.

2. To help men become more Christ-like by leading them to examine their lives more closely in order to discern their progress — or lack of progress — on the road to

---

* Chapter VIII's "Looking At The Same Picture"

spiritual maturity, and then making the necessary corrections in order to experience continuing spiritual growth.

2.   A CHALLENGING CONCEPT

You know, of course, that God's ways are not naturally our
ways, and our thoughts are not naturally God's thoughts. (Isaiah
55:8) I suppose that's why whenever men are asked, **"Husbands,
why don't you forget about trying to make your wives perfect
and instead, make it your duty to focus specifically on your own
faults and needs?"** their response is apt to be an attempt to
protect what they consider to be their role as a man.

That is neither an unusual nor an unreasonable question to ask.
Christ also pointed out that need. *"But seek* **ye first** *the kingdom of
God, and his righteousness . . . ." (Matthew 6:33a)* However, men
take the protection of their manliness very seriously.

The concept of focusing almost exclusively on their own faults,
giving up the right to point out their wives' faults, really seems to
make men bristle. Men often question the wisdom of the very idea
of not being responsible for keeping women in line. Sometimes I
get the feeling they're wondering if such a ``ridiculous'' idea is even
Christian. Quite a few men react to me personally when I ask them
to consider this concept. I think I know how Columbus must have
felt when he proposed that the world was **not** flat. A **very common** response many husbands come back with is, ``If the men you
are working with stop making sure that their wives stay in line, who
is going to make sure that those women don't become
irresponsible?''

Brother! See how that tends to reveal a very critical attitude
toward women? See how it suggests that only men are the
standard-bearers of righteousness and without men, women
would destroy all that is Christian and good? This kind of critical
thinking cannot be healthy to any relationship, much less a marriage. It denies that women are just as concerned about Godliness
as are we men, but they really are!

It also seems to imply that the Holy Spirit is unable to deal with
the conscience of a woman, and, therefore, men tend to think
they must. It is not the intent here to try to convey by any means
that women don't also have problems. But, it is definitely the intent
of this book to present a **special challenge** to men specifically; to
show that many of the problems in a marriage would not be
present were it not that husbands are creating them; and to show

husbands how to solve the problems that are bound to come up in any marriage.

This book is intended to present to men specifically some unusual challenges that will develop a closer walk with the Lord. A man needs a relationship with the Lord that will provide his wife with more than a dominant figure in their marriage. God wants every Christian marriage to have a Christ-like, spiritual leader, one a wife can **follow**.

There are many wives who have thought, "I wish my husband were even half the spiritual leader that he thinks he is."

It is true that a wife may realize that many people believe her husband to be a spiritual giant, but she knows that others can think that only because they don't have to live with him and see him as he really is. Still other wives recognize their husbands to be better than most, but also know that there's still much room for improvement.

I guess one more sad thing is that too often a wife can't even tell her husband that these really are the thoughts of her heart because she fears his reaction. She is concerned that he can't handle even constructive criticism, and she doesn't want to hurt him. I know my wife has had these thoughts about me.

MAN, THE ESCAPE ARTIST

You know it really is amazing how we men can get so busy making sure that others don't foul up, that we don't have the time or desire to examine our own lives more closely. This unequal form of justice seems to be noticeable in relationships between husbands and wives specifically and men and women generally. Just how glaring that unfairness is in many men's thinking towards women will be graphically demonstrated in the following illustration taken from a life situation.

Frank was **frequently** and **deeply involved in gross immorality**. Yet, even with this sin in his life, on many occasions he would insist, yes, even demand that his wife, Sue, be **very careful** that she not violate **any** of her obligations as a Christian. She must **always** be absolutely submissive to him, no matter what. Often he felt the need to scold her. What was Sue doing that caused Frank to feel (in spite of his own grossness) that he must draw attention to her faults? What glaring fault of hers so successfully distracted him from his wrongs? What caused him to become so concerned about how she was violating her obligation to scripture?

She was very angry and, in an emotional state, she would scream at him because of his infidelity. Contributing to her lack of self-control was the fear that she was possibly being subjected to venereal diseases.

Ironically, Frank, having initiated the offense, actually said that he felt that he could not, "in good conscience," allow Sue to go on unchecked in **her** irresponsibility. Although Frank says he is a Christian, he still finds it more convenient to overlook his responsibilities and makes his **top** priority pointing out his wife's failures.

This may be considered an extreme example to some; however, as time goes on I'm finding this attitude to be a very common one. Because it is so common, the following is a point that needs to be considered carefully. I have been surprised as I watched those who, having heard about what happened in this marriage, looked at what Frank did, heard about Sue's reaction, and then passed right over the grossness of Frank's sin to actually make comments like, "It's not right for her to get angry!"

Certainly you and I know anger is not God's goal! But, let's step back for a moment and observe this situation. Doesn't it appear strange that anyone's focus would specifically narrow in on Sue's anger while ignoring Frank's sin? In the interest of at least an equal evaluation, doesn't it seem like a gross miscarriage of justice? The scales are out of balance . . . But why?

Let me give another comparison: (This example should further illustrate the injustice involved in men's singling out women to magnify their wrongs.)

Greg discovered that Larry, a close friend, had come over to Greg's house to visit him. Finding Greg gone for the evening, Larry forced himself on Greg's wife. When Greg came home and discovered his wife had been violated, he became violently enraged at Larry, purposing to wreak vengeance upon him. The average man would feel that Greg was justified in becoming outraged at Larry.

Can you see any similarities in the illustrations? In both situations there was **anger at immorality** and **rights violated**, but Sue was condemned for her anger while Greg became the champion of justice when his anger burst forth.

This tendency to demand that wives be absolutely responsible, while husbands give themselves the freedom to be irresponsibly unaccountable, is not new to men. It is illustrated time after time, even in the Scriptures.

I suppose one of the most striking examples of this is found in John 8:3-11. Let me see if this particular scene can be brought into focus. Picture Jesus standing with a small group talking over a few things. As they are talking, he notices a commotion down the road. They're a little far off to tell what it's all about, but it looks like a mob scene with some of the "Religious" leaders in front. It also looks like they might be dragging someone along with them as they approach. Yes, they are. They're dragging someone with them! As they are coming closer, the crowd following the action gets bigger and bigger. By the time the mob reaches Him, Jesus is able to see that they've been harshly forcing a woman to come along with them. The "Religious" leaders responsible for this scene are really indignant about something.

Keep in mind that these leaders have been out to discredit Jesus. We find now that they are prepared to trap Him with a loaded question. They say, "This woman was **caught in the very act** of adultery . . . Moses says she should be stoned; what do you say?" Pressed for an answer, Jesus replies, "*Let the person without sin throw the first stone.*" What a sobering effect this has on their "righteous indignation"! Having been stopped by His words, they begin disappearing, one by one, leaving the woman behind.

Now stop and reflect for a moment on this story: Caught, in the very act . . . isn't adultery a two-person sin . . . ? Where was the man?

Why didn't they drag him down to be stoned? It really wasn't justice they were concerned about after all, was it? It seems, that even from long ago men have had a tendency to reserve for themselves preferential treatment, without realizing the destruction it can produce in the spirit of a woman.

I feel, and I think the facts reveal that women tend to have much more sensitive spirits than men do. (You might call it tender heartedness or being emotionally sensitive.) Also, I feel that when wrongs have been committed, a woman's conscience will in most cases bother her **much more**, than a man's conscience will bother him.

For instance, in the case of Frank and Sue, Sue will **suffer** much more than Frank will. Although Frank may feel the pressures of being discovered, and of his wife making him accountable with her angry responses, Sue will feel **more guilty** because **she got angry** at him even though she had the right to do so. She will blame herself for his unfaithfulness. "I must have failed; why else would he have strayed?" is apt to be her attitude. She will feel inadequate as a woman, wondering why she couldn't keep her man happy. But no man can accuse anyone or anything for **his** own unfaithfulness.

> *"But every man is tempted when he is drawn away of his own lust, and enticed." (James 1:14)*

> Wives often do get angry at the offensive attitudes and behavior of their husbands. And husbands usually react in anger to their wives' emotional outbursts. The solution is not husbands defending themselves. The solution is for husbands to change their offensive attitudes and ways.

3. ARE YOU LETTING RICHES PASS THROUGH YOUR FINGERS?

Are you able to identify and understand the lessons God is teaching you?

> *"Therefore I speak to them in parables because seeing, they see not and hearing they hear not, neither do they understand . . . for this people's heart is waxed gross. And their ears are dull of hearing and their eyes they have closed lest at any time they should see and should understand with their hearts and should be converted and I should heal them." (Matthew 13:13-17)*

We can sometimes be so blind to the lessons God is bringing. He is trying to teach us through circumstances that He allows to exist in our lives. Rather than learning His lessons, many times we resent, react or overlook them.

There were circumstances in my life that needed interpretation if I were to discover God's lesson in it for me. In looking back at them perhaps the "principles of examination" and "right interpretation of circumstances" in our lives will be more clear.

Picture this scene: It is National Secretary's Week, and we have fifteen secretaries working with us. There are only a few of us men and the boss has just announced that we are going to honor the secretaries by taking them out to lunch. There are about four girls to each car and the men are to drive them to the restaurant. My home is directly across the street from the office and down about one block. Furthermore, my wife Nancy, who loves to mow the lawn, is not only out mowing the lawn, but she is standing next to the street when I pass by with a carload of happy secretaries. Since she knows them all and they all know her, quite naturally they all joyfully holler, "Hello!" "Hi, Nancy!" etc., as I'm driving by.

Are you getting the picture? A perfect setting for jealousy to flare up. Nancy thinks to herself, "Don't get jealous now. He's only following orders. He can't help it. Jealousy is wrong." Etc. Etc. But, all that rational thinking does not help her. So, she prays; she reads her Bible; she argues against her jealousy. She purposes not to take it out on me.

Along about 5 o'clock she feels like she can handle it. When five-thirty comes and I walk through the door, the whole world blows up in my face. You know how they say that ignorance is bliss . . . well, I couldn't speak for the bliss part, even though I suppose I could plead ignorance. I stand there in all my innocence, shocked, with a questioning look on my face that says, "What did I do?!"

THE RIGHT RESPONSE FOR ONCE

As I stand being attacked and my defenses are being activated, I can do the **normal, usual, righteous** thing, and be well within my rights. Anyone would agree with the rightness of these so-called normal, righteous responses that I might use. But, **I would be the loser!** I would miss learning two very rich lessons through this situation which God allowed to happen especially for **my benefit.**

Some of the normal responses to my wife could have been:

1. *"Aren't you ashamed of yourself for being jealous?"*
   Certainly she was! She didn't need any more criticism.
2. *"You certainly are a bad witness."*
   She knew that too; more accusations were unnecessary.
3. *"Boy! are you unfair; you know I had no control over the situation. What do you expect me to do about it?"*
   She knew she was unfair; that's why she was reading her

Bible and praying. If she couldn't help herself with her own problem, why should I dump more misery on her by asking that question?

Notice the two valuable lessons that God was offering to teach me:

1. How to discover the thinking in a woman's mind that develops jealousy.
2. How a man can meet the needs in his wife's life, causing her to have such confidence in herself and her husband that jealousy would no longer be a problem.

Had I not learned these two things* and ministered to Nancy, she might not have come to the point of being able to enjoy the meaningful, lasting friendships with those secretaries that developed.

Every man should learn these two lessons in order to build — and, if necessary, even restore — his marriage.

THE PROBLEMS SUMMARIZED:

1. Husbands do not generally understand the minds of wives.
2. Husbands are inclined to be blind to their own faults but quick to condemn their wives for their faults.
3. Husbands don't always know how to evaluate the circumstances in their marriages from God's perspective in order to use those circumstances as building blocks.

Many men do not know how to make the change from just seeing what is happening to also seeing what God is teaching through what is happening.

Hopefully, the illustrations and examples, situations and circumstances presented herein will clearly present these three basic problems and will also offer solutions to those problems. God has lovingly provided for us a blueprint (His Word) that is invaluable to men who are seeking to become Christ-like and to build — or possibly rebuild — their marriages.

CHAPTER FOUR

DISCOVERING
A WOMAN'S MIND

To do this, your spirit must become alert to the spirit of your wife. Does your marriage indicate that you are a husband with or without this alertness?

GOING A HUNDRED MILES AN HOUR ON THE WRONG TRACK?

God's institution (marriage), with man's reasoning to govern it, will fall short of being a complete and genuine success.

It is not unusual to find that, when there are personal problems between a man and his wife, the man, thinking he knows the solutions, tries to apply **his** solutions. When **his** solutions do not work, he may become frustrated. He may even seek help from others. When he sees that the "normal solutions" don't seem to relieve the situation either, he may give up, thinking that since the answers **he** has do not work, that there are no answers to marital problems. He may conclude that a man must learn to accept a "miserable marriage" as normal or get out of it.

Unsolved problems in a man's home, especially those between him and his wife, tend to cause him to feel frustrated and to wear down his endurance, possibly causing him to lose interest in the marriage and to not care about his wife. IT IS NOT, HOWEVER, PROBLEMS IN MARRIAGES THAT ARE THE REAL DIFFICULTY. IT'S **NOT KNOWING HOW** TO SOLVE THE PROBLEMS. THAT'S WHAT WEARS A MAN DOWN!

A problem is a doorway, offering us the opportunity to enter into understanding. Solutions which are derived from within the **natural mind** often prevent problems from leading to blessings. We need to learn how to look at problems from God's viewpoint. But that skill must be learned because God's ways are not naturally man's ways. (See Isaiah 55:8)

"All the ways of a man are clean in his own eyes: but the Lord weigheth the spirits." (Proverbs 16:2)

"Every way of a man is right in his own eyes: but the Lord pondereth the hearts." (Proverbs 21:2)

"When left to himself . . . Every man did that which was right in his own eyes." (Judges 21:25b)

MAKING MATTERS WORSE

Most men do not have the slightest suspicion that many of the husband-wife problems they are facing are problems that they have actually created all by themselves! Experiencing problems over which we seem to have no control is difficult enough. Why would anyone want to create more problems for themselves? It is interesting to note that many men do indeed create more problems for themselves even by doing what "seems right." You see, there is a way that **seems right to a man** but the results will be destruction (See Proverbs 14:12 and 16:25). It would profit us greatly to learn how to reflect upon our circumstances from God's perspective rather than from our own. We must learn how to benefit from our circumstances, not be victims of them. WE WILL BENEFIT FROM OUR PROBLEMS ONLY AS WE **CHANGE** THE WAY **WE** LOOK AT THOSE THINGS THAT ARE GOING ON IN OUR LIVES WHILE THEY ARE HAPPENING.

DO WOMEN CONFUSE YOU?

Paul said. *"Let this mind be in you, which was also in Christ Jesus."* (Philippians 2:5)

And the ability of the mind of Christ is revealed in the following verses: *"But when Jesus **perceived their thoughts,** He answering said unto them . . . "* (Luke 5:22)

The woman at the well said to her neighbors of Jesus. *"Come, see a man, which **told me all** things that ever I did: is not this the Christ?"* (John 4:29)

Isn't it inspiring and motivating to think about developing the capacity that Jesus had to be aware of what others were thinking? Even women!

BECOMING SKILLED

Something specific happened that confirmed this principle and made me aware that it really is possible to know, without my wife saying a word, what her innermost thoughts are within a given situation.

One Saturday when Nancy and I were painting the front room, my friend Gary came by to invite me to go with him to K-Mart. Trying to learn to be a considerate husband, I said, "Just a minute; let me check with Nancy." I went inside and asked her what she thought about my going to the store with Gary. She said, "Sure, that's okay, go ahead." Going back outside, I told Gary, "You go on, I'm going to stay here. Thank you for asking me to go with you, though."

When my wife heard the door open a few minutes later, she was surprised. "I thought you left with Gary. Did he change his mind about going?"

"No," I replied. "I didn't go because you didn't want me to." With a slight smile, she quizzed, "But, how did you know that? I thought I had hidden how I really felt!"

She had done a good job of trying to conceal her true feelings from me, so how did I know? The answer to that question is simple. Simple to know now, yes, but it was very difficult to learn how to detect her true feelings. Difficult, because it required more of me than I thought I would have to pay in order to learn it. Oh yes! the answer to her question . . . I saw how she really felt, IN HER SPIRIT.

I have since learned most women do not like to appear to be "the boss". A wife would rather her husband not ask questions in front of others which make it look as if she were making the decisions. It is possible to learn her opinions without creating an embarrassing situation. Ask while alone with her or at least make sure your question does not draw attention to her or her answer.

Most women are concerned that they will be thought of as stubborn, strong willed, or dominating if they state their true feelings or wishes. They also may fear that expressing themselves truthfully will result in a fight. So, often, they won't speak up. I think they usually are more willing than are men to surrender their rights.

In this case, as you may recall, my wife and I were painting the front room, supposedly together, and I was leaving her to do it alone.

Too often a man doesn't place enough value on his wife's spirit: he doesn't recognize that God wants to teach him through his wife to become sensitive to the spirit of others. When a man does not recognize and receive the messages being sent to him through the spirit of his wife, he fails to benefit from these learning opportunities.

Maybe, like me, you have received signals from your wife, but ignored them as worthless; often those are signals that God has sent you through your wife. He is trying to make you more sensitive, especially to areas that your wife sees in your life that need improvement.

I know that I could have gotten away with being upset at my wife for what could have been viewed as her selfishness about my time. I could have let her know, too, that I felt like she was trying to run my life and that I didn't like it. But, **I would have been the loser again!**

God desires that all husbands stop being losers. He wants us to be able to perceive the spirits of our wives and of others. He wants us to keep the problems in a marriage from intensifying or compounding. He knows that problems, allowed to continue, can destroy a marriage.

"*But he that doeth wrong shall receive for the wrong which he hath done: and there is no respect of persons.*"
(*Colossians 3:25*)

If a husband is to be the spiritual leader, his spirit must be sensitive to spiritual things. He must be sensitive to God's spirit prompting his spirit. Before he can minister effectively to her, he must also be sensitive to his wife's spirit. A man should become so alert to the spirits of others that he can discern the emotional state of another, sometimes even over the phone.

The apostle Paul's spirit was so alert to the spirits of others that he sensed that the spirit of a certain woman was not a good spirit even though she proclaimed Paul to be a servant of God. (Acts 16:17-18)

> If you are a "new" husband and your wife already has the following problems, you will need to know how to help her. If she does not have these problems, it will profit you to know how to keep them from developing.

Here are some typical problems which may show up in a wife and are indicators of a husband's need to become skilled as a spiritual leader:

1. She is a stubborn, strong-willed wife.
2. She is a domineering wife.

3. She is emotionally unstable; she often seems to be angry, crying, or fearful.
4. She has sexual problems.
5. She has lost interest in her Christianity.
6. She is losing interest in her personal appearance.
7. She lacks confidence in herself or her abilities.
8. She is a jealous wife.
9. She is a poor communicator; talks too much, doesn't talk, gossips, or is thought of as asking too many questions of her husband.
10. She is experiencing excessive depression.
11. She is unable to accept herself or others.
12. She has attitudes of spiritual superiority toward others.
13. She appears to be resisting the grace of God and seems spiritually weak or uncertain.
14. She doubts her salvation.

Can you imagine how most men would respond to the suggestion that the foregoing problems could be traced to their failures as spiritual leaders. Some husbands, even right now, are probably thinking the same thoughts that I've heard expressed by so many other husbands. That is, I've heard them express such thoughts until we sat down and closely examined the causes and effects of the problems in their marriages and then examined how husbands, as spiritual leaders, should go about resolving those problems.

Some husbands have remarked, "If you knew my wife, you wouldn't say that I had failed. She had those problems **long** before I ever met her." That statement prompts me to ask, "How long have you been married?" With a puzzled look on their faces, as if they were wondering why I would ask that question, the average husband may reply, "four years." (The time factor is not the determining factor of this question.)

Answering my next question perhaps allows them to feel they can prove they have not failed. "Since you were married, has she gotten better or worse?" They usually shoot back without hesitation, "Worse!"

I then ask. "If you are the spiritual leader and the job of a spiritual leader is to bring the one you are responsible for to spiritual maturity, then why has she gotten worse, instead of better?"

If things have gotten worse in your marriage and you're trying to think of reasons why they have gotten worse, consider your leadership. Check the preceding list again. Are there traits you should be ministering to?

Wouldn't it be to your advantage to learn one way to discover when you are on the wrong track, especially if you could discover it without anyone having to say anything to you and then be able to correct it yourself? Consider the following:

A Secret To Understanding The Spirits Of Others, That Women Practice Often; Some, Without Even Knowing It.

Next time you are with some couples, try this little experiment. It is designed to let you see this secret in practice.

Ask a husband a question **about his wife**, then **watch him** as he answers you. In turn, ask his wife a question **about him**. Then **watch her** as she answers you.

A suggested question to the husband might be, "Do you think you spend as much time talking with your wife as **she** would like"? A suggested question to the wife might be, "Does your husband give you **quality** conversation time where you can share your innermost feelings?"

Notice anything special when they answered? When he answers the question about his wife, the average husband will usually **look only at you**. But, the wife will be **very watchful of her husband** while she is answering you. Why do you suppose that is?

If you performed this experiment, you saw something take place that women do naturally. It happens every time women are dealing with people. Even though it is a common thing, you may not recognize it; you might not be able to identify it, even as it is taking place right before you. Do you know what to look for?

Here's what you should be noticing: Women watch for attitudes. They observe the spirits of people by noticing facial expressions and voice tones. As the wife in this experiment answered you, she was watching her husband closely, to see what his response to her would be. Often she will base her answers on what she feels **he would be willing to hear** her say about him. That's because it's so very important to a wife that her husband **does not** reject her. Sometimes it is easier for her to live with an answer that is not the truth than with his rejection.

On the other hand, as the husband answered you, he was watching **you** more than his wife, because, too often, what others think of him is more important than what his wife thinks of him. He is, in most cases, not even thinking about how his words or ways might affect his wife or others. Most men don't even realize that everyone has a spirit and that they must be careful to not wound or damage the spirits of others. *"The spirit of a man will sustain his infirmity;* **but a wounded spirit who can bear?**" *(Proverbs 18:14)* Wounding the spirit of a person is a good way to create an enemy.

Has your wife ever said to you after leaving someone you had been talking with, "You turned them off" or "You offended them!" or "They weren't listening to you!"?

Did you believe her? Or did you ignore her? If you ignored her, that's too bad. I used to ignore my wife, too, until I learned how much I was hurting myself by not paying attention. You see, wives are noticing something that we men are not normally noticing.

Remember when I said that many men are actually creating for themselves a lot of the problems that they are facing? This is what I meant: often men are not as alert to the spirits of others as they should be. A man with an insensitive spirit will be unaware of hurting the feelings of others. If a man is not alert to the fact that he is hurting the feelings of those he is dealing with, he shouldn't wonder if he finds himself in difficult situations, situations that might never have developed if he were more sensitive. He might have avoided unnecessary, hurtful words or actions if he knew what to watch for.

THE NEED FOR A SENSITIVE SPIRIT

It is absolutely essential to a healthy Christian life that we have a very sensitive spirit. It is our unseen spirit that is able to come close to the unseen Spirit of God. The spirit does not have flesh and bones. (Luke 24:39) It's like the wind; you know it's there but you can't see it. (See John 3:8) We can only feel as close to God as our spirits are alert to sense God's Spirit. It is through our spirits that the Holy Spirit communicates with us. *"The spirit itself bears witness* **with our spirit.**" *(Romans 8:16)*

Jesus was able to live a sinless life because his Spirit was in direct communication with the Holy Spirit of God. He was able to know and do the will of God.

> *"For I came down from heaven, not to do mine own will, but the will of Him that sent me. (John 6:3) I do nothing of myself; but as My Father has taught me, I speak these things. And He that sent me* **is with Me;** *The*

Father has not left me alone; for I do always those things that please Him." (John 8:28,29)

WOULD YOU LIKE TO BECOME SENSITIVE?

As mentioned earlier, it often doesn't even occur to us men to think about others having a spirit. We don't think about ourselves having a spirit either. The first step then would be to become aware of the concept of a spirit: God's, ours, and other's. This will require that a man change his way of thinking. A significant step in becoming alert to the spirits of others is to stop resenting one's wife and the things she is saying and doing. She should be seen as a mirror in the hand of God, showing us how sensitive or insensitive we are to her spirit. A man can only successfully minister to the spirit of his wife or to the spirits of others as his own spirit becomes sensitive.

A husband can gauge the sensitivity of his spirit by asking, "Am I meeting the needs of my wife's spirit?" If she is **unpleasant**, I am not meeting the needs of her spirit. If she is **pleasant**, I am meeting the needs of her spirit.

"A merry heart maketh a cheerful countenance; but by sorrow of the heart the spirit is broken." (Proverbs 15:13)

"A merry heart doeth good like a medicine: but a broken spirit drieth the bones." (Proverbs 17:22)

At this point, a person can mentally argue with this principle or learn from it. A husband should learn to give totally of himself, loving his wife as Christ loved the Church; the husband should always be striving to present his wife holy, decreasing her character flaws by his good example. (Ephesians 5:25-29)

A man cannot learn to understand the mind of a woman without also recognizing the need to understand her spirit. When a husband decides to become sensitive to his wife's spirit, it will cause his own spirit to become more sensitive. Because his spirit's sensitivity is increased, he will be able to have increased fellowship with the Spirit of God, receiving more clearly instructions from the Holy Spirit and God's Word. No man can even say that Jesus is, in fact, his Lord if he is not being **led** by the Holy Spirit. (I Corinthians 12:3b)

As a means of becoming alert to my wife's spirit, a very helpful project for me was to learn to watch carefully her eyes and facial expressions. It is very hard, though, to develop this habit. Many of us have been conditioned since childhood to avoid eye to eye contact. Because, as children, if we saw others disapproving of us, we learned to look away instead of trying to change our ways.

Something you might want to be alert to is this: if you let your wife know, as I did, that I didn't like it when she disapproved of my offensive ways, your wife will try to hide her true feelings from you just as my wife did from me. Because my looks of disapproval made Nancy feel that I was rejecting her as a person, she stopped wanting me to see her expressions of warning or caution or her feelings of grief or anger. Even though most of the time she was trying to help protect my reputation, my insensitivity was causing her to suffer. Because it hurt her too much to feel my rejection, it became safer for her to let me fail. I remember a very important lesson God taught me through a poorly hidden look of disapproval from my wife. This lesson too, made me aware of how delicate the feelings of a woman are.

We had been visiting with a friend in his place of business. Several girls were working for him. After our visit, we got into our car. As I got ready to start the car, I looked over at Nancy and noticed a very severe expression of resentment on her face. I asked. "What's the matter?" "Nothing," she said, with a tone in her voice that meant, "Don't play dumb! You know what's wrong and I'm not about to get into another fight with you by telling you!"

In the past, had she said. "Nothing," when I gave her a chance to express herself, I would have thought to myself. "Well, you had your chance, Toots!" Then I would have proceeded with whatever I was doing. Again, **I would have been the loser!**

But, this time, having learned to value what God wants to teach me through my wife, I insisted, "We will not move until I know what is bothering you." Finally, with concern about what it was going to cost her in additional suffering, she said, "I don't like the way you were flirting with those girls in there!"

"Flirting?!" I threw back in a high pitched voice. "I was just being friendly!" I explained

She still insisted. "I'm a girl and I know what flirting is to a girl, and that was flirting!"

Having become aware that God was helping me see the need to re-evaluate my life and attitudes, and even though it was very difficult, I paused to consider her statement. Feeling it would be good to search my heart in this matter, I thought to myself:

Q. What was your motive?

A. I was just trying to be friendly.
Q. How were you being friendly?
A. Well, I was being funny and wanting to be clever.
Q. Why did you feel the need to be clever?
A. Well, what's wrong with wanting to be clever and "cool?" Everybody wants to be thought of as "neat." It's nice to be the center of attention.
Q. Why do you need to be the center of attention with other women?
A. Doesn't every man feel good about girls paying attention to him . . . ?

Yep! she's right: that's flirting! For sure! I had to admit to her that her evaluation was accurate. I have tried since then to never act toward women in a way that my **wife** would interpret as flirting. I would try to not ever again rely on how I might interpret what is or is not flirting. My conscience is not always willing to judge me accurately. Without Nancy helping me, I might not have known the **difference** between paying **Godly attention to the spirit** of a woman, and, paying **special attention to the woman.** That's one of the causes of jealousy!

Paying special attention to a woman will tend to build a man's own ego instead of building in the woman an awareness of Christ-in-the-man. It's a tragic thing to watch husbands flirt with other women in the name of "Christian Friendship" and to see wives suffer guilt feelings because they are experiencing jealousy. Often wives do not say anything about how they feel, because so often the husband justifies his actions, turns the situation around, making her appear to be the culprit, the criminal. It's as if he is saying to her, "How dare you have such unfair, unrealistic feelings?"

When a husband is friendlier with other women (smiles more, listens better, helps more, is more courteous to, etc.) than he is with his own wife, it could be very easily, and legitimately, thought of as flirting. It certainly can be considered being more attentive, and it will very likely create jealousy within his wife. Should anyone receive more special attention from a man than his wife?

A man can be with a friend or other men who are flirting and experience temptations. Seeing a friend getting all those friendly smiles and cute little looks because of his clever flirty ways can entice a man to join in the "fun," perhaps not even realizing what he has done. It's very natural for men to see that kind of excitement and want to be a part of it. He doesn't have to plan it; it just happens. That's why **we must be on guard** to watch out for and avoid getting caught up in situations that are not wholly pure.

"The lips of the righteous know what is acceptable . . . "
(Proverbs 10:32)

"Let the words of my mouth and the meditation of my heart, be acceptable in thy sight, O Lord, my strength and my redeemer." (Psalms 19:14)

"Set a watch, O Lord, before my mouth; keep the door of my lips." (Psalms 141:3)

*"My son if thou wilt receive **my** words, and hide **my** commandments with thee; So that thou incline thine ear unto wisdom, and apply thine heart to understanding; Yea, If thou criest after knowledge, and liftest up thy voice for understanding, If thou seekest her as silver and searchest for her as for hidden treasures; Then shalt thou understand the fear of the Lord, and find the knowledge of God, For the Lord giveth wisdom: out of his mouth cometh knowledge and understanding. He layeth up sound wisdom for the righteous: he is a buckler to them that walk uprightly. He keepeth the paths of judgment, and preserveth the way of his saints. Then shalt thou understand righteousness, and judgment, and equity; yea, every good path. When wisdom entereth into thine heart, and knowledge is pleasant unto thy soul: **Discretion shall preserve thee, understanding shall keep thee;** To deliver thee from the **way** of the **evil** man, from the man that **speaketh froward things;" (Proverbs 2:1-12)***

*"As obedient children, not fashioning yourselves according to the former lusts in your ignorance: But as he which hath called you is holy, so **be ye holy** in **all manner of conversation;** Because it is written, Be ye holy; for I am holy." (I Peter 1:14, 15, 16)*

The next chapter is designed to help a man see from a woman's perspective how a marriage disintegrates.

CHAPTER FIVE

CARING

FOR A WIFE

Have you ever wondered why wives seem to have more emotional problems than husbands do?

When they were first married there was laughter, a longing to be close to one another, and excitement. Now it's gone. The feelings they once had for each other gradually disappeared. Where did it all go? What happened?

Before continuing, as a means of gaining a meaningful frame of reference, ask anyone who has spent any time at all working with marriages: "Who do you think is more desperate about the success or failure of their marriage: husbands or wives?" Most will tell you that wives are overwhelmingly more concerned.

A wise pastor once told me that a meaningful service to men would be to find a way to let them recognize the serious trouble for which their marriage was headed. He shared that he knew of twenty-five couples in his church whose marriages were headed for destruction. But, he also shared that he didn't know how to get the couples to see it for themselves. You see, he knew how defensive men can become when shown their faults.

This pastor was not saying that men purposefully want to defend anything that is wrong. Instead he was saying that because men can be insensitive to their wrong attitudes or actions they often, blindly defend something that is actually wrong.

Why do men become so defensive when they are asked to examine themselves? Scripture says that no one likes to have their wrong ways exposed. They don't want light shed upon their evil.

"And this is the condemnation, that light is come into the world, and men loved darkness rather than light, because their deeds were evil. For everyone that doeth evil hateth the light, neither cometh to the light, lest his deeds should be reproved. But he that loveth truth cometh to the light, that his deeds may be made manifest, that they are wrought in God." (John 3:19-21)

The questionnaire which appears on the following pages was designed to reveal areas that a man needs to examine in order to evaluate himself and consider what effects his answers will have upon his marriage.

Because a husband's attitudes, actions or words will be significant factors in his wife's life, it is essential to understand how much control, yes, control, a husband has over his wife's emotional condition. Most husbands do not realize how much influence they have over their wife's emotional stability, whether she wishes him to or not.

16 ATTITUDE INDICATORS

CHECK ONE . . .

Yes	No	Often	Seldom	
☐	☐	☐	☐	Would your family say that your work habits make your work seem more important to you than your family? (Ecc. 2:4-11, 5:12, 13; Prov. 15:27)
☐	☐	☐	☐	Would God be pleased with all that your eyes look at and how long you look? (Job 31:1)
☐	☐	☐	☐	Do your children look at you as a wise teacher? (Prov. 17:6b, 15:2; Deut. 6:7)
☐	☐	☐	☐	Does your wife feel that after your relationship with God, she holds **first** place in your life?
☐	☐	☐	☐	Do you **seek your wife's counsel** before you make decisions (as much as possible)? (Phil. 2:2; Matt. 19:5,6; Eph. 5:31)
☐	☐	☐	☐	Do you think your wife is **too emotional?** (I Peter 3:7; Prov. 18:14)
☐	☐	☐	☐	Do you look forward to talking with your wife with as much enthusiasm as you experience when talking with friends (or even strangers)? (Mal. 2:14,15; John 15:15)

Yes	No	Often	Seldom	
☐	☐	☐	☐	Do you share your inner-most needs with your wife for her to pray for and with you? (I Pet. 3:7; I Tim. 2:1,2)
☐	☐	☐	☐	Do you welcome her criticism of you as an opportunity to evaluate how you affect others? (Prov. 21 :2; 17:10; 27:5; 15:31,32)
☐	☐	☐	☐	Do you know the goals of each member of your family? (Prov. 27:23; 22:6)
☐	☐	☐	☐	Does your wife confide her secrets to you? (Prov. 14:26)
☐	☐	☐	☐	Do you get angry at members of your family? (Prov. 14:29; Eph. 6:4; I Cor. 13)
☐	☐	☐	☐	Do you think of your family members as "ones God has given to help you learn"? (Phil. 2:3)
☐	☐	☐	☐	Would your wife say you put her spiritual and emotional needs above your sexual needs? (Matt. 6:33, II Pet. 1:3-6)
☐	☐	☐	☐	Do you feel that a home, money, or prestige build security in a wife? (Prov. 16:25; 24:3,4)
☐	☐	☐	☐	Would your wife say that you understand her frame of reference in most matters? (I Pet. 3:7)

Do you know that many women fiercely resent that men actually have so much control over the emotions of women? I cannot over-emphasize the extremely serious responsibility God has given us concerning the care of our wives, to become to her a living illustration of Christ.

A VERY IMPORTANT REMINDER:

> Again, we mention that this book is addressed specifically to husbands and seeks to place the responsibility squarely on men to become **adequate Spiritual leaders.**

Let's take a look at what is happening in so many "average" marriages:

1. A man and woman get married, anticipating happiness.
2. Gradually, little things that demonstrate thoughtfulness or kindness seem to be forgotten or overlooked by the husband. Possibly he doesn't even know about such things.
3. The wife is hurt by this neglect, but still she is willing to give him the benefit of any doubts, concluding that he is tired or busy, or that it was just an oversight on his part.
4. She doesn't say anything about his neglect though, because it seems too "picky".
5. Even with time he doesn't seem to improve. Rather, his thoughtlessness seems to increase.
6. As time goes on, he even seems to become less sensitive toward her, becoming very selfish.
7. If she reminds him of how he used to be more loving or that she wishes he would become more loving, she gets the feeling from his attitudes or actions that he doesn't care. He doesn't seem to share her enthusiasm for a mutually joyful relationship. He seems to project the attitude, "You live your life, I'll live mine." Or he may project the attitude, "Everything seems just fine to me; you're just **looking** for trouble."

8. Though she is really searching for ways to restore or even build the oneness that is so **vital** to her emotional well being, he sees her need to talk about their problem as nagging.
9. Her spirit is wounded even more now. She interprets his attitudes toward her as personal rejection.
10. She soon recognizes that he is more concerned about her response to him sexually than he is about her feelings. Not only is he NOT "living with her in an understanding way," but as she tries to explain her needs, she finds he really doesn't want to learn.
11. She feels disloyal and guilty because she's reacting to him and his insensitive manner towards her.
12. She becomes openly unstable emotionally.
13. Realizing their marriage is in trouble, she asks him if they can get help.
14. He, having seen her emotional instability, responds. "I don't need any help; you're the one who's having the problem. If you want some help, go get it for yourself, but don't bother me with your problems anymore."

Restoring relationships in a marriage seems to be much more important to women than to men. Women usually see and feel the effects of problems first, which means a wife will have been struggling with it much longer than has the husband. Wives often put much more effort into finding solutions. They are more often the ones who are reading books, going to seminars, seeking counsel etc., etc. Often, a husband either unknowingly or stubbornly refuses to acknowledge the depths of the responsibility that he **does** have for his wife's spiritual and emotional condition. **A husband's refusal or inability to responsibly manage his role of spiritual leader will add to and increase his wife's emotional instability.** Sometimes it will even cause her to question her sanity.

Because so many husbands do not seem to know how to lead their wives to spiritual maturity, not only in extreme situations, but even in normal every day situations, they find their wives attempting to find their own solutions.

Depending on her personality, she may choose any one of the following as her course of action:

1. The "No Problems" Wife

This wife may resign from being an active participant in the marriage, becoming a passive member, merely performing her duties as necessary. This passiveness will add to the feelings of guilt she has been experiencing. Though her spirit is drained of strength to continue the struggle of caring about her marriage, she knows that giving up is not the answer. She may feel she has become a liar or an actress, **playing** games, pretending everything is fine in her marriage, even when she knows it is not!

Then because her husband is not manifesting love and concern for his wife she will come to **resent** the feelings of "being used" sexually by her husband.

Too often, a husband is not even aware his wife has given up on their marriage. Some husbands think everything is fine simply because their wives have quit complaining.

After years of living in this manner wives sometimes decide to end the farce and often husbands are shocked when their wives announce they are tired of playing the marriage game, that they are leaving or have found another romance. A wife who has come to this conclusion finds her guilt is almost unbearable, but she's determined to make the new situation work somehow!

I'm not saying this is right. I'm only explaining what **is** happening.

2. The "Dying Inside" Wife

One of the deepest longings of this wife is to know that her husband needs her. Instead, she sees that he is indifferent to her. To a woman, that's the same as personal rejection.

Of course, that type of rejection will cause her spirit to be wounded. (Do you know that if you continue to cause others to hurt emotionally, it is certain that you will be causing their spirits to suffer also? Most people never seem to tie the two, spirit and emotions, together.) Sooner or later, her wounded spirit will start to affect her emotions. She will start to show signs of being emotionally disturbed. As might be expected, this will cause her to seek help, probably starting with the reading of books. Just reading books will allow her to keep her unstable condition a secret a little longer, but eventually she will feel the need to come out into the open for help.

And each time she finds a new approach, she will think she has received "sure cure" instructions, steps for her to follow. Each time her hopes are raised, because she thinks, "Now I have answers that will allow me to rise above my emotional dependency." But her hopes are dashed again and again because the instructions she received which were designed to give her emotional freedom don't work for her.

Stop and think about it. How could they work? The steps were designed to work for her, not for her husband. Yet her emotional hurts are coming from her husband's problem: insensitivity. Her husband has a disease and she's taking the medicine.

Still, she can't stop blaming herself for failing. She thinks she is over-reacting. She feels guilty for taking his indifference so personally. As a result of this continuing "treatment-failure cycle", her emotions will usually become increasingly unstable. The see-saw of having hope, then watching her hopes dashed, seems unending. She knows her husband is disturbed with her condition, but her grief is further intensified when she begins to hear that their friends are disturbed about **her.** Also they're wondering how a husband can be so patient and tolerant under such trying circumstances, living with that "poor sick" wife. **She** is seen as an emotionally sick wife, and **he** is seen as very stable.

This wife's guilt and wounded spirit will probably start showing itself in physical illness. The kinds of physical ailments these types of wives can experience are limitless.

3.   The Silent, "Spiritual" Wife

This wife has heard teaching which emphasizes that it is unspiritual for a woman to have **any** expectations of her husband. So, because she does not want to be unspiritual, she stops **openly** expecting her husband to demonstrate husbandly characteristics. But, **inwardly** she still longs for her husband to have Christ-like **love for her.** Because she really does still want him to appreciate and admire her, she feels unspiritual and this adds to her guilt.

Many people are not sensitive enough to notice that the spirit of another is being squashed. Because her mouth is not speaking words of discontent, others who know her assume that everything is alright (I Peter 3:1), not realizing that she is, in fact, in agony and anguish inside in her spirit. A quiet spirit is not just a quiet mouth.

It is not at all eccentric, crazy, or unusual for any wife to want her husband to be alert to the fact that she is a person, to demonstrate to her, in words or actions and especially in attitude, that **he needs her**, too! But she has been taught to think it is eccentric.

It shouldn't be asking too much for a Christian husband to be Christ-like toward his wife.

So now, this wife who has been told that the "good Christian" thing to do is "give up her expectations" is still trying to stop wishing that her husband would love her. She looks **outwardly,** placid or undisturbed, while **inwardly** she's eaten up with emotional turmoil. She feels even more like a hypocrite now since she is pretending everything is just fine when she knows it isn't. Everyone considers her a spiritual giant, so more than ever now, she certainly can't let them know the truth. She can't cry out for help. She not only feels trapped; she is trapped.

4. The "Strong-Willed" Wife

This wife is generally more outspoken than a lot of women. She is also becoming more resentful and bitter because her marriage circumstances are becoming more hurtful each day. Many times now she has talked with her husband about his offensive ways and it has just made him resent her. He saw her outspokenness as her refusal to be submissive. So now she starts letting others know about his failures.

She probably is embarrassed about others hearing that he is not attentive to her, but feels it's worth being embarrassed if it will cause him to experience some humiliation too. She may even want to tear him down out of vengeance. (Again I'm not saying it is right for her to do this. I'm just pointing out particular responses in wives that need to be resolved.)

Now this wife will have to learn to live with the knowledge that she has been branded a "strong-willed-woman" because she is letting others know that her husband's irresponsibility as a husband is hurting her. How unfair that she should have to bear this brand all alone!

5. The "I-Guess-I'm-Not-So-Bad-Off" Wife

An interesting fact about so many wives is their capacity to be extremely loyal and unselfish. They can think they are being too demanding for simply wanting things to be better. I know there are many husbands who will refuse to believe the preceding statement, but it's still true. There are many wives who though not wanting to, do settle for marriages that are far short of what they could be.

I can best present this type of wife to you with the following illustration: Although our acquaintance was only brief, I felt very comfortable with a certain couple. After some friendly conversation, we gradually came to a point where we were talking specifically about their marriage. She was the first to break the ice. "I feel kind of ridiculous for wanting to get together with you. I guess it's because we don't really have any situations in our marriage that are desperate. Even though our marriage isn't exactly terrific, it isn't terrible either. Maybe that's why I feel guilty and ungrateful. I feel that I'm expecting so much from my husband," she said, evaluating herself. "He really is a good man," she added.

Wanting to let her know that I understood how she was feeling, I asked her if I could express what I thought she was going through emotionally. I hoped to say to her husband for her what was in her heart in such a way that it would give him a new look at his responsibility as a Christian husband. She gave her permission. Looking at her, I said, "You say to yourself, 'Even though our marriage seems to be missing something spiritually, when I look around at other marriages, I see that I'm really not so bad off. My husband is a good provider. He has good friendships. He's never left us. He follows through with his responsibilities around the home. He's a reliable business man. He's a good father. He doesn't neglect the children. He never physically abuses us. He makes sure that we attend church regularly. He helps out when the church needs him. He reads his Bible...what more can I expect of him?' " I concluded.

She nodded her head as if to say, "Yeah!"

Again, speaking for her, I said, "What more can I expect from him?" Quickly adding "perfection!?" Realizing that those had been her thoughts, her head dropped down as if she were ashamed of herself. Speaking for myself now I added, "What do you expect

from a Christian husband? That he be like Jesus . . . Perfect?"
Understanding now the point I was making, she lifted her head
slowly, looked at me with a slight smile that said, "Yeah, I see what
you're saying now."

I continued, "Is it such a terrible thing for a wife to be unwilling
that her husband be anything less than what God desires for him?
"Christ-like! If God designed a wife to help her husband be
successful, would He design her to be satisfied with helping him
become anything less than Christ-like?"

Her husband realized that he should accept, as an honest need in
her, her longing to have a more Christ-like example to follow. This
husband challenged himself to quit playing around and to get
serious about discovering what God was showing him through her,
to learn how to be more sensitive to her spirit and to the Holy
Spirit.

Here is another brief example of a wife settling for less, because
she was making faulty comparisons:

This wife's father never bought her anything other than what he
felt was absolutely essential. He made her feel stupid, ugly and
unwanted. He also hit her with his fists. Her husband on the other
hand never hit her. He bought her clothes, even though he liked to
use them to show off his wife's figure to prove to others with his
trophy, that he was a "real man". However when they went
places, he often used her as his source of humor. She didn't feel
good about a lot of things he was doing, but she didn't dwell on
them because she reasoned that she had never had it so good. This
kind of reasoning does not benefit husband or wife nor does it
challenge a husband to become more Christ-like.

Unfortunately there are thousands upon thousands of wives
who have come to any one of the preceding conclusions. Some
wives have come to drastic conclusions and their husbands don't
even know it. Not hearing from their wives about these concerns
can cause husbands to unknowingly lose the privilege of seeing
and resolving these problems in their marriages.

It is heartbreaking to realize that wives believe their husbands
actually do know how they have hurt them. Wives think that their
husbands just don't care about how they are being emotionally
destroyed. Wives don't realize that most husbands **really don't
even see or know what they are doing to their wives.** Wives don't

understand how ignorant, yes ignorant, we men tend to be about the need to be sensitive to the spirits of our wives or to the spirit of anyone else, for that matter.

It is difficult for me to convince wives that when a husband asks, "What did I do?", that he really doesn't understand what he's done. Because his offenses are so very obvious to her, she finds it hard to believe that those same offenses are not obvious to him also. Therefore, a wife can become very bitter.

Because of all this turmoil in their marriages, some wives develop a very strong sense of self-preservation in order to survive. Wives who came from homes where they had stable family lives or who have a great deal of personal confidence can survive longer than others. Even though severe damage may have been inflicted upon their spirit causing scars they will carry for life, these more confident wives seem to be able to continue to hang on to their sanity longer. Even though suffering, they still try to carry on as growing Christian ladies, leaving their husbands immature and far behind. In no way is he a spiritual leader. His wife becomes, in fact, the spiritual leader.

> We know that divorce is not a part of God's ways. However, did you know that even though a great number of couples may not believe in going through the legal process of divorce, that many times they are IN FACT, divorced, spiritually, emotionally and physically!

I know that reading these illustrations which place the responsibility and pressure for marriage problems and failures on men will cause a severe reaction in some men. That's normal. In fact, the average response would probably be something like this:

"It sounds like **all** the blame for unsuccessful marriages is being put on the man and I can't accept that! That's not right! A wife doesn't have to react wrongly toward her husband! The grace of God is sufficient for wives too, you know!"

PLEASE, LISTEN! IF SHE'S WRONG, YOU KNOW HER RESPONSE IS NOT GODLY; I KNOW HER RESPONSE IS NOT GODLY; SHE KNOWS HER RESPONSE IS NOT GODLY. If you, for example, were to ask her while she were angry, "Do you know that your anger is wrong?" she might respond with, "Yes, you idiot, I know I'm wrong!!" She may even be spiteful enough to refuse you the satisfaction of knowing that she realizes she's wrong. That's part of the nature of anger. In fact, her knowing all this is part of what is eating her heart to pieces, heaping even more guilt upon her already heavy spirit. **But is that all you want to do, point out her wrong response? Do you want to let Satan be successful in using her anger to distract you, or do you want to resolve the problems?** Remember, we are still focusing exclusively on husbands, asking them to examine the contrasts between themselves and Christ **first**. This attitude will help restore a wife.

Should **our** responsibility for a Godly marriage stop because we don't feel that our partner responded properly? Should we be so determined that our wife be scolded for her improper responses that we allow the very circumstances to continue that are causing her problem in the first place?

To further illustrate, is the preceding attitude not similar to expressing anger at our child for coming into the house with a stab wound and bleeding on the carpet. All the while we're scolding him he's dying. And yet we justify our wrong response with "After all, a carpet really was not made to be bled upon, was it?"

Wouldn't it be even more cruel if (as is often the case) the one who did the scolding were also the one who did the stabbing? Considering everything, wouldn't it be better to do away with the stabbings? Then we wouldn't have to deal with the bleeding on the carpet.

That's the whole idea! Helping a husband to see how he is stabbing the spirit of his wife. If a husband were to quit stabbing the spirit of his wife, he would no longer have to scold her because her emotions were bleeding all over their marriage. Remember we talked about husbands creating problems for themselves? This is just another example.

If you are anything like other husbands you may realize that we all are basically unable to love our wives the way God does. That's why God has to tell us **how** to love our wives. God says in essence,
    *"Husbands, because your ways are not My ways, use
    Christ's unselfish love for mankind as your example of
    how to love your wives." (See Ephesians 5:25-29)*
If we do this, we will cause our wives to become spiritually mature through our loving examples.

One husband said, "Are you trying to say a perfect husband makes a wife perfect?" My reply was, "I don't think we have to worry about that possibility."

Still insisting, he pursued the question, "If Jesus, being perfect, had had a wife, are you saying then, that since He was perfect, His wife would have been perfect?"

Although, I was noticing the not-too-uncommon attitude of scorn he was showing toward women, I said to him, "Since Scripture commands me to make my first priority that of actively seeking how I might become Christ-like, a better question would be: if my example, Christ, had a wife that was a miserable, rebellious, strong-willed, angry wife, would He have stopped being Christ-like?"

He had to acknowledge that this new perspective needed to be his priority.

LIKE IT OR NOT

Whether we as husbands are willing to acknowledge it or not we are much more responsible for the spiritual, emotional and physical condition of our wives than we might think! We may not want that responsibility. But, we do not have a choice. It's like signing a contract to join the army. Once we've signed it, we're committed. The same is true of a marriage. In the army, if more is required of us than we expected, that's too bad for us. The difference between a commitment to the army and a commitment to marriage shows up when it comes to having to follow through with that commitment. The Army can force us to honor our commitment; a wife can't. And husbands know that.

Once I'm married, as far as God is concerned, I'm accountable for the success of my marriage. The position of husband carries with it the charge of being spiritually responsible. The two cannot be disconnected any more than can living and breathing. They go together. My responsibility and relationship to my wife is to be just as Jesus' responsibility and relationship is to the Church. (See the illustrations on pages 54 and 55.)

One pastor said to me, "Whenever I heard the expression, 'laying-down-your life,' I always equated it with being willing to die for my wife, like the marine who jumped on a grenade, killing himself, preventing his friends with him in the foxhole from dying. And of course, I have always said, 'Yes, I would gladly be willing to die for my wife.'

"But you're talking about something else here. You're talking to me about learning to put my wife first in our marriage, about trying to meet her needs, even before meeting my own needs. And if it comes to a situation where it's just a matter of opinion between my wife and myself, to give her opinions priority over mine. In other words, putting consideration for my wife before myself in our everyday living. Boy, that's going to be rough!"

It is impossible for me to gain real understanding about the innermost feelings of someone else if I am preoccupied with myself. It's something like not being able to receive into my hands some gold coins because I'm so worried about losing my copper pennies that I won't open up my hands for the exchange to take place.

One man said, "I feel like you're asking me to lose my identity, as though I'm not supposed to be **me** anymore."

"Exactly!" I replied. "That's what becoming Christ-like means: I'm not me anymore, because I'm being conformed to the image of Christ." Galatians 2:20 says, "*I am crucified with Christ: Nevertheless I live; Yet not I, but Christ liveth in me. . .*"

Another verse says, "*If you have any encouragement from being united with Christ, if any comfort from his love, if any fellowship with the spirit, if any tenderness and compassion, then* **make my joy complete** *by being like-minded (Christ-minded), having the same love (As I have for you), being one in spirit and purpose, (Christ and I). Do nothing out of selfish ambition or vain conceit, but* **in humility consider others better than yourselves,** *(Philippians 2:1-3) (New International Version)*

As I try to make these verses become a part of my life, to free myself from being preoccupied with the faults of others, it helps me to think of others as those whom God is using to teach me, to show me, regardless of their methods, how to become more Christ-like.

After all, isn't it only fair for me to first become a living illustration of what I want my wife to become?

Ephesians 5:25 says, "Husbands love your wives even as Christ also loved the Church and gave Himself for it.
The following illustration describes Ephesians 5:25-29

1

THE CHURCH

2

CHRIST   THE CHURCH

3

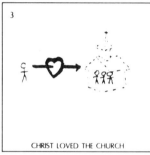

CHRIST LOVED THE CHURCH

4

CHRIST DYING   THAT THE
TO SELF, PROVING   CHURCH WOULD
HIS LOVE   BECOME GLORIOUS

5

OTHERS SEE THIS GLORIOUS CHURCH
AND ARE WANTING TO EXPERIENCE
THIS RELATIONSHIP TOO

6

OTHERS RECOGNIZE THAT WHAT THE
CHURCH IS, IS A RESULT OF CHRIST'S LOVE;
SHOWN BY HIS NOT LIVING FOR HIMSELF,
BUT, DYING TO HIMSELF.

7

OF COURSE CHRIST ACKNOWLEDGES
THAT HE WILLINGLY DID THIS OUT OF
ABSOLUTE OBEDIENCE TO GOD

**LIKEWISE,
YOU
HUSBANDS
LOVE
YOUR
WIVES.**

The illustration of Christ and his bride, the Church; substituted now, with a husband and his wife. (Ephesians 5:25)

1

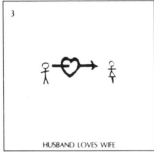

WIFE

2

HUSBAND   AND WIFE

3

HUSBAND LOVES WIFE

4

THE HUSBAND DIES TO SELF, PROVING HIS LOVE   THAT THE WIFE WOULD BECOME GLORIOUS

5

OTHERS SEE THIS GLORIOUS WIFE AND ARE WANTING TO EXPERIENCE THIS RELATIONSHIP TOO

6

OTHERS RECOGNIZE THAT WHAT THE WIFE IS, IS A RESULT OF HER HUSBAND'S LOVE SHOWN BY HIS NOT LIVING FOR HIMSELF, BUT, DYING TO HIMSELF.

7

OF COURSE, THIS HUSBAND ACKNOWLEDGES THAT HE IS WILLINGLY DOING THIS OUT OF ABSOLUTE OBEDIENCE TO GOD FOLLOWING CHRIST'S EXAMPLE.

THIS IS GOD'S BLUEPRINT FOR A SUCCESSFUL MARRIAGE. IT IS A HIGH CALLING AND A SERIOUS RESPONSIBILITY.

CHAPTER SIX

LOVING
HER AS A PERSON

Do you realize that your wife
may have more reason to be
concerned about your
character than you do?

WOMEN ARE PERFORMING HEART SURGERY ON THEMSELVES

Women tend to blame themselves when something goes wrong in their marriages. A wife may, at first, focus only on her husband's offense, but, usually, after thinking about it, she will end up feeling that she is, after all, the one who is wrong, even when she has been absolutely right. That's why books, seminars, workshops, etc., for women are so widespread. Women are looking for ways to improve themselves.

The object of this chapter, though, is to reveal to men ways in which they wound the spirits of their wives and to show how women whose hearts are hurting will try to reprogram their hearts, trying to convince themselves that that which hurts their hearts does not really hurt or at least should not hurt.

Too often men simply will not allow women to hurt. A woman expressing her hurts is just not acceptable to many men and so women, wanting to be acceptable and feeling guilty for hurting, try to reason away hurts by saying to themselves, ``I'm wrong for being too sensitive.''

A wife will often feel guilty, too, for even letting her husband know he is hurting her, but not being honest about the hurt will not bring improvement into a woman's life. It is in fact, an unrecognized attempt to change God's design for her as a woman. It will produce emotional turmoil to take that course.

Too often men don't have the slightest awareness of how they hurt their wives. The following are examples.

A DESPERATE NEED

As I stood talking with a couple, the wife expressed that she didn't know that she wanted to even think about her husband meeting her needs anymore. She related that for years she really had longed to know **he needed her** but it had begun to seem hopeless that he would ever express such a need. When she would ask, ``How did your day go'', he would reply impatiently, ``Okay.'' Then he would hurt her more by evidencing a lack of cooperation and an unwillingness to become involved in conversation about his day.

At another time if he were doing something and she would ask, ``Can I help you with that?'', he would answer ``No, I'll get it myself'', causing her to feel as though he thought she would ''mess it up''.

Then, if he did want her to help him, it seemed as if all he did was get upset or impatient with her, making her feel as if she couldn't do anything right. So many times, when she tried to enter into his life, he made her feel inadequate or excluded. Those attitudes (which he was unknowingly demonstrating) were killing her inside. She knew how much she **NEEDED** him (that is, his acceptance of her was **vital** to her) . . . But, she said, ''He doesn't need me!'' So, she looked elsewhere for some purpose to her life, for something to distract her from feeling unneeded, something of interest to make her feel valuable and worthwhile.

> I'm not saying these things are wrong or that every woman doing these things has a husband who is not meeting her needs. I am, though, pointing out what women often do hoping to feel valuable, needed, or accepted. Some women are even desperate enough to respond to other men who make them feel needed. These things cannot make a woman feel fulfilled. It is God's design that only her husband can meet her need; only he can make her feel accepted and fulfilled as a wife. That's why it is so devastating to a wife when she doesn't feel her husband needs her.
>
> Since they cannot produce lasting results, these other methods can produce severe anxiety in a wife.

Trying to stop the hurts, women try tennis, swimming, jogging, and other sports; women's Bible studies, either as a participant and/or leader; or by becoming active in social groups; finding some way to help or serve others, sometimes, even something like babysitting. Many wives want to go back to school, often to prepare for independence ("I can't count on him anymore, so I'd better start counting on myself"). Then, finally the wife begins to work in an attempt to find something and/or someone to whom she can give her loyalty and dedication.

As a response to this wife's expressing that she didn't feel her husband needed her, her husband said, "No, you're wrong; I really do need you!"

I said to him, "What you just said to your wife didn't help her; it only hurt her even more."

"You just said to her in effect, 'If those are your feelings, then your feelings are not right. They are untrustworthy. You are wrong again because you have falsely accused me.'"

"I told him 'It's not a matter of whether or not you think she has come to the right conclusions. But it is, definitely a matter of, **did** your ways cause your wife to feel that you, in fact, did **not** need her.'"

> A husband who wants to learn how to meet the needs of his wife **must** learn to accept what she feels. Her words are legitimate expressions of her heart. Christ lets us come to Him and share whatever is on our hearts! And He does not make us feel rejected when we do. (James 1:5) We need to allow our wives to feel that same comfort. (II Corinthians 1:4)

A man must come to a point in his life where he realizes that his wife **needs** to love him, care for him, become a part of him. She also **needs** to know that he feels as if he is a better man because of her love for him. A man needs to learn how to receive his wife's love. I wonder how many men know how to do that?

DISASTROUS FUN

He thought it was great fun, but it was destroying his wife! He was only teasing, he insisted. But tears were still streaming down her face. Then, because he insisted he was only teasing, **she** felt terrible for being so "temperamental." Thinking about her problem, she rationalized that no other wives are hurt by silly comments the way she is. I assured her, though, that millions of other wives are hurting too because of the same careless, insensitive comments that other husbands are making.

This is what happened:

While watching T.V., a commercial came on that showed a stewardess pampering a male passenger. Because his wife knew he had traveled by airplane and because she knew he was getting ready for another trip, she asked him if the stewardesses really paid that much attention to the men passengers. He, thinking it would be great fun, began to tease her by assuring her that they did. Then he started building a story about how much they had paid special attention to him in the past. This wounded her spirit, causing her to think that her husband allowed other women to pay such special attention to him. Since so many women, no matter how attractive they are, feel they can't compete with "Miss Universe" or the "ideal woman", teasing about other women scares them. It's unfair, because it is threatening. It causes them to wonder if they are going to be able to keep their husbands. It does nothing to help a wife's self image. Even the "Miss Universe types" feel insecure about their ability to attract and **hold** a man.

Too many husbands are enjoying the spotlight at gatherings at their wives' expense, telling jokes about them. Wounding the spirit of a wife with cutting humor, publicly or privately, is attacking her character and will cause her to feel rejected as a person. It is such a common thing in marriages to use the wife as the source of humor that many have the impression it is alright to do so. It may, however, be deadly. I'm talking about little events that are funny between a husband and wife that are told to get a laugh at her expense. A woman may even laugh the first time the "joke" is mentioned, but it ceases to be funny after awhile. It is bad enough for husbands in general to do this, but it is especially grievous when a Christian husband does it.

> We husbands cannot allow ourselves the freedom of careless comments. It is irresponsible to even take the chance that our words might cause our wives grief. It is essential that our words minister grace (Ephesians 4:29); that our words are healing (Proverbs 12:18; 15:4, 23; 16:24). If our words hurt, then we must stand accountable for them. We cannot allow pride to stop us from letting God use our wives to help us change conversational habits that demonstrate carelessness or insensitivity to her or anyone else.

I remember a wife who threw a bar of soap away because it had gotten ''dirty'' after it had been used to wash some greasy hands. The very idea is funny since almost everyone knows that the soap could have been washed clean again, but her husband should never have repeated this story to others without her permission (which, I feel, should not even have been sought).

Telling stories about her will cause a wife to think that her husband's goal is to prove to others that she is stupid. That doesn't cause her to feel accepted and approved by her husband. It's not a good idea to ask her for permission in public either; that puts her in a bad light too. The best policy is to never say or do anything that will belittle a wife in the eyes of others. If she wants it to be known, then let her do the telling.

THE CRIME OF CRYING

There are many reasons for crying; some legitimate, some not. Many wives, however, do not feel the freedom to be honest with their feelings. Many hide their true feelings, not letting their husbands see them cry. Why would women resist the God-given, emotional expression of tears?

There were three wives sitting across from me in a restaurant, and I overheard them talking. Although I didn't hear all of the conversation, I did hear one of the girls, with bitterness in her voice, say, "It really hurts me when he does that."

Her friend, understandingly, said, "When my husband does that, it just kills me too."

The third girl questioned. "What do you do when they do that to you? Do you cry?"

In defiance, the second girl said. "Are you kidding? I wouldn't give him the satisfaction of knowing that he hurt me."

The third girl wondered again, "How do you keep from crying?"

The second girl answered, "I just won't let myself!" Call her refusal to cry stubbornness if you like, but the fact is, she didn't feel free to be honest about her feelings with her husband!

I know of another situation where a husband was being very cruel to his wife, emotionally. His words to her were equal to a beating as far as she was concerned. A couple of times I saw tears start to come into her eyes, but she didn't cry. Later, letting her know that I saw her about to cry, I asked her why she hadn't.

She said, "I felt myself about to cry, so I had to get control of myself quickly."

"What's so terrible about crying?" I asked. "Oh! I can't let him see me cry. It makes him mad!"

Do you know how common it is for women to force themselves to develop the habit of "not crying?" Very common! It really disturbs a lot of men when their wives cry. There are men who would actually beat their wives if they were to see them crying.

Before I realized the significance of crying, it used to frustrate and irritate me too. I remember one time during a quarrel when my wife started crying, I told her, "If you're going to cry, then get out of here. Go to the bedroom and stay there until you can quit acting like that." Can you see, as I do now, how poor my attitude was?

Why do you suppose crying disturbs so many men so much? I think one reason is because they don't know how to handle it. I also think that in some cases it produces instant conviction in a husband for his wrong attitudes, actions or words. Most men do not like that kind of accountability.

Crying is the result of an emotion. Emotions are part of God's design. You can tell a lot about the condition of a person's spirit through his emotions. If you see **joyful emotions**, then the **spirit is joyful**. If you see **grieved emotions**, then the **spirit is grieved**. That's what the Scriptures say!

"*A merry heart maketh a cheerful countenance; But by sorrow of the heart the spirit is broken.*"

(Proverbs 15:13)

A good spiritual leader is alert to the spiritual and emotional conditions in his marriage and ministers accordingly.

"*Be thou diligent to know the state of thy flocks . . .*

(Proverbs 27:23)

It is grievous to realize how many women think it is wrong for them to cry. Grievous, because the pressure of holding in emotions will show up, somehow, somewhere.

Women sometimes decide they cannot cry because:

1. Some have heard it said that women use tears manipulatively, to get their own way; so, in order that others not think that of them, they refuse to cry no matter how much they might be suffering.

2. Some have learned from parents who were angered and who may even have punished them for crying that it is safer not to cry.

3. Some think tears are a sign of immaturity or a loss of self-control. Rather than be thought undignified, they do not permit themselves to cry. Women should remember that Jesus wept!

4. Often a woman fears crying lest her husband know what hurts her and how to hurt her. Afraid of being vulnerable and at his mercy, she will not cry.

5. Some have been convinced by the accusations of others that crying is a sign of being "such a baby" or "too sensitive" or "too emotional," so even though they may be of a temperament to cry easily, they feel guilty and stop crying.

6. Some women cry because they don't feel that their husbands love them and they long for him to. But still they might try to hide their tears and their need because they think they are being too demanding.

> A wise husband will recognize that a crying wife is a wife who needs attention. Most of the time a husband should comfort his wife in these times of need.

I believe that most doctors' offices and hospital rooms would be less crowded if husbands could learn how to eliminate the physical sickness caused by their failure to meet their wives' emotional needs.

LIMITLESS POWER TO HEAL

Emotional comfort: a thing that costs no man, and is in unlimited supply.

The following is an example of the powerful healing effects upon a wife when she receives comfort from her husband.

One afternoon Chris called me on the phone sobbing so heavily she could hardly talk. She did finally manage to let me know what had happened. Some circumstances had come about that had upset her very much and she had tried to let her husband, John, know about her feelings. The more she discussed it with him, the more irritated he became. With a degree of bitter indifference, and not really wanting to hear her answer, he asked, "So whatta ya want me to do about all this?"

She answered, "I thought that you wanted to become our spiritual leader, to try to find ways to help me become more mature, to help me become emotionally stable, to heal me."

Out of frustration and resentment at seeing his inadequacy, John snapped back, "Well I can't help you, and nobody else can either. Only God can heal you!" His conclusion let her know just how hopeless and intolerable he felt she was.

Chris's question, as she was talking with me on the phone, was, "You said that he **could** meet my needs and heal me of these emotional hurts, but he says he can't. Is he right? I don't see what he can do. There is no help for me, is there?"

Since Chris had just explained the circumstances surrounding this situation to me, I was aware of three things that John could have done that would have brought her the help and healing she needed. These three things could have saved this situation from turning into a major catastrophe for them. I said to her, "Chris, I can think of three things your husband could have done."

"No!" she said, "he did everything he could have; it's just me. I really am hopeless! I really am impossible to tolerate!"

So I asked her, "Did he come to you and gently take you into his arms and just hold you?"

"No," she said, with a change in her voice and spirit that said, "I wish he had, though."

Then I asked her, "Did he let you know, that he realized that you are hurting, and that he wished you weren't hurting?"

"No." Her emotions were settling down even as I was questioning her.

Next, I asked her, "Did he let you know that, even though your emotions and actions were out of control, that he still loved you?"

Her answer, again, was, "No."

Then I asked her, "Do you feel as though you would have been as emotionally out-of-control if he had done those three things?"

"It really would have made a lot of difference if he had done those things," she reflected wishfully.

I wondered if I could talk with John so she called him to the phone. We talked for a few minutes, while I sought to let him know that I loved him and understood his dilemma, too. (It's not so uncommon for men to **not** know what to do!) I went through those same three steps with him.

Somewhat startled, he said, "And **that** will really help her?!"

"Why don't you ask her! She can let you know better than I can, just exactly how much it would mean to her."

She assured him that it really would be **very** meaningful to her.

Then, because **he** was still under pressure and wanted to avoid his responsibility (which is very common), he said, "Well, I can't do it now though! She knows you told me to do it."

I let him know that a wife really would rather that her husband could respond to her out of his own heart, but, if she knew that he was trying to learn, trying to be the husband that God wants him to be, it would be easier for her to accept at this point, that at least he was following through, even if he were following helpful hints given to him by someone else.

I remember talking with John a few weeks later. I asked him if he felt the three steps I shared with him had been helpful. He replied "I would not have believed its effectiveness had I not seen it with my own eyes!"

But this **must** become a natural, daily, consistent part of a husband's response. It is not just a one-time-application-and-you'll-live-happily-ever-after thing. A husband must practice the act of comforting regularly every time there is a need and the Holy Spirit prompts.

A man is to be to his wife as Christ is to the church (Ephesians 5:25). Wives need to be able to bring their burdens to us and have us relieve them. Jesus said that those who were laboring under heavy burdens could come to Him and He would relieve them (Matthew 11:28). And we are to have His willing attitudes about it. "Let this mind be in you, which was also in Christ Jesus" (Philippians 2:5). He is the Great Physician who loves to care for us!

HOW DEPENDENT ARE WOMEN ON MEN FOR THAT HEALING?

We had a meeting with a group of couples for a marriage workshop. Looking around to make sure that none of the other couples who were present could hear her, one of the wives asked if we could talk. Feeling safe, she expressed her concern. "I'm having a real hard time with bitterness because there is a person I can't forgive." She further explained that this situation involved another woman and her husband.

As a step toward resolving the problem, I said, "It would be important for you to let your husband know of the struggle you are having."

As if she were feeling trapped, and not wanting the trap to close on her, she replied, "I can't. It always ends in a fight when we talk about it."

Knowing that he was the key to the solution, I said. "It really is necessary that he be aware of your struggle as a first step in resolving it. Maybe, as we meet together this Thursday we can work on it." She was willing, though still doubtful, to settle for that at that time.

Thursday afternoon we met separately. After some casual conversation, this wife who had been inwardly tormented over this problem for a long time decided now was the time to bring it out. She felt more secure, because she knew someone else was there to "protect" her.

She: "I have a question about something that has been bothering me for a long time; I just can't get rid of the bitterness I have toward a certain person."

He: Angrily snapping his head around to glare at his wife, then quickly looking at me, he said with gritted teeth, "For crying out loud! Here we go again! I guess she's going to beat me with this for the rest of my life! Even though I've asked her to forgive me a million times!"

Me: While watching her husband stare into the fireplace with a look that could almost ignite the logs, I said, "In a situation like this if a wife is not able to rid herself of bitterness toward the other woman, it is usually because the husband has not done that which is necessary to replace the bitterness in his wife's heart, filling her heart, instead, with love. He has not demonstrated sufficiently that he loves his wife so much that she is free from thinking that her husband doesn't love her. In other words, he needs to cause her to exchange her mental picture of an unfaithful husband to a mental picture of a kind, thoughtful, sensitive, loving husband."

While I was keeping an eye on his wife's condition, he was still staring into the fireplace. Tears were running down her cheeks. Wanting him to see how this was affecting her I said, "Do you see how this is affecting your wife?"

He ignored me. So I said again, "You ought to see how this is affecting your wife." His eyes sliced across the room to his wife, then back to the fireplace. I explained. "She's really hurting." I knew it would be important for him to **see** how destructive his **past** irresponsible ways were, how they affected his wife's **present** emotional and spiritual condition. This could cause him to be cautious about his ways **now** to guard against **future** consequences.

He: Still ignoring her. "Well I'm really fed up with this thing!"

Me: "There are some things you could do to put an end to
      this, to restore your wife's inability to forgive and to lead
      her to a place of greater spiritual maturity as you be-
      come more Christ-like, too."

He: (Very bitterly, and, as if to escape his responsibility)
      "Well I've tried everything I know how to do, and she
      still won't get off my back. I don't know what else I can
      do!"

Me: Trying to show him specifically that there was more he
      could do, I said, "You could get up and go over and hold
      her in your arms and let her know that you care that she
      is hurting. That would show her that you do care."

He: Still sitting there, he said, "When you've tried everything
      you know how, what else can you do? I want her to
      realize that she's not been so perfect either!"

Me: "Isn't it interesting, how stubborn we are. We say we
      don't know what else we can do, and when we learn of
      something else we can do, we still won't do it.
         He said later. "That word **stubborn** hit me like a ton of
      bricks." But, that afternoon stubbornness was still win-
      ning. I paused for a while to see what he would do. He
      sat there doing nothing, so I said very emphatically,
      PLEASE. . .LET ME EXHORT YOU, GET UP AND GO
      OVER AND HOLD YOUR WIFE!"

He stood up. As he did so, his wife stood up too. He went over
and embraced her. She stood there in his arms, emotionally
expended, crying for several minutes. I was crying too. I left the
room for a while to let them be alone. A little while later when I
went back in, I discovered his wife had left the room to "fix her
face."

While talking with her husband again, it seemed important to
point out to him another very significant fact about women.

"It would be very important for you to be aware of something
that took place here just now. Please mark this down in your mind
as a valuable aspect of understanding your wife. A woman needs
acceptance from her husband almost more than she needs food.
Evidence of the **desperate** need in your wife for **your** acceptance
of her is demonstrated in this: even though your wife knew that I

had **forced** you to embrace her, she still accepted your embrace. That's how much she needed to know that you care for her."

You know what's exciting: This wife today is rid of that bitterness and is full of loving forgiveness, because that husband is replacing his lack of understanding with understanding. He's doing that by listening, as his wife let's him know what and how he can minister to her heart. He has convinced her that he needs and wants her to help him understand her. He's learning how God would love his wife through him, and she is responding! God's ways are always dependable and trustworthy!

The next chapter reveals more problems that are happening in typical marriages. The goal is not just to identify problems, though, but to illustrate them clearly enough so they can be understood and resolved. Also, to put forth the principle that if a man can get to know his wife well enough, he can be watchful for that which will minister to her even before she might feel the need to tell him about it. This eliminates quarrelsome fighting with her.

CHAPTER SEVEN

A NEW WAY
TO SEE AND HEAR

> Have you thought of listening
> to and looking at yourself
> through your wife's eyes and
> ears?

ARE MEN BLIND AND DEAF?

One of the joys we are experiencing is the privilege of working with couples in small groups. In these groups, husbands are purposing to learn how they can become more Christ-like and are setting for themselves the three goals we mentioned in the first chapter.

In these groups we discuss the various needs within marriages. There are times when comments are made which reveal needs within the marriages of those present. Those needs range from the normal to the very severe.

One of the goals of these meetings is to interpret for husbands what wives are saying. In addition to meeting as a group, we also have the special opportunity of meeting with those same couples individually in their homes. On one such occasion a husband was asking to be shown how he could improve his attitudes and responses toward his wife. Quite unconsciously he was doing and saying things that were very devastating to her. I was helping him examine the things he was doing to her at the very time they were taking place. Even though he was seeing it, it was still hard for him to adjust his thinking to the idea that those things he was being shown were actually wrong, especially since many of those things are normally acceptable in many marriages. It is always interesting, though, to see what God will use to help men to **experience** understanding. This time was no exception.

Since this particular group of couples had been meeting for a while, this husband had had time to observe some of the other husbands in the group. Reflecting upon their ways, he said of two or three of them, "I can't believe some of the things these guys say and do to their wives and not know it. Do you really think that they don't see what they are doing?"

Assuring him that it definitely was possible, I nodded my head yes.

He was quietly thoughtful for a few moments. Then, with an inquiring look of concern on his face, he said, "Could it be that I am also blind to ways I am hurting my wife and that its just as clear to others what I'm doing? Are they watching me, too, and wondering how I can be so insensitive?"

"Yes," I nodded my head again, sympathetically. What a blessing it was to watch the Holy Spirit deal with that husband's spirit, causing him to see and understand in his heart the facts concerning his ways and the destructive effects some of them were having on his marriage. It wasn't as though this husband was a beast; he was just doing what comes naturally to most men.

Here's another illustration of how men can be blind to their offensive ways. Marie was telling me how her friend Sharon was being tormented by the insensitivity of her husband Mark. One day Marie decided that she wanted to help Sharon. She outlined a plan to Sharon who readily agreed to it. Marie was to illustrate to both Mark and Sharon a difficult and harsh marriage situation she knew of (even though Marie had already told Sharon this story). It was supposed to be a hint to Mark about his own harshness. The stage was set, so Marie told "them" about a pastor whose wife was expecting a baby and how unconcerned this pastor was to his wife's needs.

As the story unfolded, Mark became more and more irritated at this "monster" of a pastor. "He should be brought before the governing board of the church," Mark protested. "A man like that shouldn't be in the pastorate," he declared.

Because of Mark's reaction, you might think that what the pastor Marie told about was doing was just short of inhuman. The deeds of the pastor were not really all that abnormal. They were really quite common. Most men are doing the same things regularly. We've all done them in one form or another. They fall under the label of insensitivity.

Marie mentioned that Mark never did notice the look on Sharon's face that said "I can't believe you can get so upset about someone else's insensitivity and still be so insensitive yourself." The last time I heard Sharon was still struggling with Mark's insensitivity and harshness.

That concept of outlining a situation in order to emphasize a point reminds me of a familiar Bible story:

King David had been having an immoral relationship with his neighbor's wife, Bathsheba. Because he wanted it to continue, he arranged for her husband Uriah to be put in the front lines of one of the heaviest battles his soldiers were fighting. As hoped, Uriah was killed. Nathan the prophet, led by God to confront King David, went to David with an illustration to help him **see** his wrong. Posing it as a real story, he told David of a rich man who had great herds of sheep, yet one day when he wanted a celebration, he decided to feast upon the one and only ewe that his poor neighbor owned. This poor neighbor had invested his love and life in the ewe. She had been very precious to him, and now the ewe was slain.

Hearing this, King David became enraged. He pronounced judgement: The rich man is a beast and should be executed because of his offenses. But, before his death, he should be made to pay back fourfold what he had taken.

"*Thou art the man!*" declared Nathan. Nathan had been **used of God** to cause David to *see* his **own** wrong. David was properly confronted and convicted. (II Samuel 12:1-7) David was rich and had many wives. Uriah was poor and had only one wife. David took for his own selfish pleasure the one and only, deeply loved wife of the poorer man, Uriah.

Incidently, you might wonder what that pastor was doing that seemed to bother others more than it bothered him. Just small things! Waiting till the last minute to get the baby's room ready . . . Agreeing with his wife on a specific color of paint she preferred and then coming back with a different color . . . Using the money for the baby for other things and saying, "Don't worry about it; I'll pay it back." Which was probably true. But it still was draining his wife emotionally.

Because of his behavior, she did not sense that he cared about her, the baby or his responsibilities to them. Sound familiar? It sounds like the type of things I've done myself.

Of course, you could say he was busy with his ministry and that's why he was so late in getting things ready.

You could also say, "Big deal! So he got a different color. What's so important about one color."

Or, "So he changed his mind; He's the boss, isn't he?"

Or, (and this is really common), "All she ever does is nag about money. She should learn to trust the Lord!"

A husband who has had those thoughts is very normal. But, such actions and thoughts still show selfishness and insensitivity. If we are loving, we look for ways to lighten the load for our wives, not add to their burdens.

"*Giving honor unto your wife, as unto the weaker vessel*" (I Peter 3:7)

A man who tries to make it a greater priority to correct his own deficiencies instead of pointing out his wife's faults will understand how difficult that is to do. Remember, "every man **thinks** he's right in his own eyes" and it's not always easy for a husband to look at his marriage from his wife's point of view.

I'm not saying a wife is never wrong. Rather, I'm challenging **men** to respond to their wives' wrongs the way Jesus would - in love -

without a condemning or critical spirit and after having first examined themselves.

It would appear there is a definite need to point out to men their inadequacies before they are able to recognize and **feel** what effects **their** ways are having upon others. Surely this is one of the purposes of Scripture in the lives of Christians.

"*All Scripture is given by inspiration of God, and is profitable for doctrine, for **reproof,** for **correction,** for **instruction** in righteousness.*" (II Timothy 3:16)

Scripture also points out that it is not unusual for us men to be insensitive.

"*Therefore I speak to them in parables because seeing, they see not and they hear not, neither do they understand . . . for this people's **heart is waxed gross** and their ears are dull of hearing and their eyes they have closed, lest at any time they should see and hear and should **understand with their heart** and should be converted and I should heal them.*" (Matthew 13:13-17)

It is essential to see ourselves as we are before we can become the completed product that God planned. We must see ourselves as we really are before we can become better equipped to serve Him.

"*That the God of our Lord Jesus Christ, the father of Glory may give unto you the spirit of wisdom and revelation in the knowledge of him: The eyes of your **understanding being enlightened** that you may **know** what is the hope of his calling and what the riches of the Glory of his inheritance in the saints and what is the exceeding greatness of his power to us-ward who believe.*" (Ephesians 1:17-19)

There certainly is a great need for more understanding between men. But there is an even greater need for increased understanding between husbands and wives.

A man should be able to discern the feelings of his wife's heart, and maybe even of others, so well that he could know how they feel even if he only hears them talking in another room.

How does a man start to develop that kind of sensitivity? In the first place, it is necessary to know that many people are not truthful about how they feel - especially wives. When asked, "What's wrong with you?", they will quite often say, "Nothing," when the truth is that they simply may not want to face the battle they expect to take place if they are honest. It may be especially threatening to a wife to consider being honest with her husband about what he is doing that hurts or offends her.

Even when a husband asks his wife, "What's bothering you?" she still knows that, in many cases, it is safer not to be honest with him. A sense of futility causes many wives to finally, after arguing for hours, give up and even to tell their husbands, "You're right," even when it is obvious to her and to others as well that he really is wrong. He thinks he has finally convinced her that he is right and that she is wrong. Evidently he's not mature enough yet or sensitive enough to realize that he has not really been victorious. But because of his stubbornness, she has given in, letting him remain a loser!

I wonder how many men have lost their jobs because they would not pay attention to their wives. Wives sometimes try to help their husbands see more clearly character flaws for which their husbands are being reprimanded on their jobs, but because husbands often feel wives are too "dumb" to see that he is not wrong, arguments and fights result. Wives may even be accused of being disloyal, because husbands think wives are taking the boss' side. Therefore, even though they were trying to help, wives frequently feel guilty and, as a result, they stop trying to help and just sit back and wait for the inevitible to happen.

Husbands refuse to make needed corrections, lose their jobs and still insist they are not wrong!

Many men are ruined financially and are suffering needlessly because they rejected important cautions from their wives. I remember that my wife didn't feel the freedom to let me know about the problems she saw in my plans and schemes. She knew from past experiences that I was not a good listener. She feared the consequences of being honest with me.

Whenever a wife fears being honest with her husband, (as my wife was) it is necessary for a husband to start listening with his eyes. Men need to learn to watch for expressions on their wives' faces that could reveal feelings that they have but probably won't express in words. It is a wise husband who learns to enter into his wife's heart by listening to her tones of voice.

I had to learn to start listening attentively to my wife when she was talking, not only as she was talking to me, but even as she was talking with others. Something I really wanted was for the two of us to become one. I wanted to know the what, how, when, where, and why about my wife.

Men who respond in anger to their wives lose out on so much. If a woman is a whiner, her husband can accomplish so much more by finding out what is making her whine. If a man sees his wife raising her lip in a slight snarl or other demonstration of disgust with him, he is often tempted to yield to anger or to defend himself. It is far better to find out what can be done to change her opinion of him. We ought to be peacemakers not heartbreakers.

"Blessed are the peacemakers: for they shall be called the children of God." (Matthew 5:9)

That's what I wanted to be; I wanted to study the expressions of my wife. I wanted to know her disposition almost as well as I knew myself. Men who challenge themselves to become authorities on understanding the unspoken messages their wives are sending will learn at the same time how to be just as understanding of others too.

BECOME AN INVESTIGATOR

If a man hears his car making a peculiar noise he checks it out. It becomes a concern to him. If he sees smoke near his home, he investigates. If he hears reports about an undependable product, he tends to be cautious toward it. Awareness of such things helps avoid failures. Since that is true, how much more should he learn to be as alert and cautious to potential problems in his marriage?

BLIND AND DEAF
TO DOUBLE STANDARDS?

Men also tend to be blind and deaf to ways they change the rules to suit themselves, but wives know how notorious men are with double standards. Consider this example:

A wife says she needs new sheets but her husband says, "We don't have the money right now; you'll have to wait till next month." Or "What have you been doing with all the money I've been giving you, anyway? No, you can't have any more to waste!" Then . . . he goes out and buys something really **essential** like a jogging outfit or another fishing pole or fancy wheels for his fancy (non-family) car or a bigger carburetor for the boat. In the meantime other **"non-essentials"** such as sheets or shoes for the kids have to wait. Men don't seem to be conscious of the fact that even though the kids' feet grow, shoes don't.

Wives can tell of many situations like this and some that are even more disturbing, but because so often husbands are not willing to examine their faulty reasoning, they have quit telling them of their injustices. Because men won't listen, learn, and change, they carry this characteristic of unfairness with them wherever they go. What advantage is there in maintaining that kind of characteristic?

Another illustration of rule changing:

My friend wanted to buy a motorcycle, and I suppose there's nothing wrong in that, but the only way at the time he could justify it was by saying that it was "really cheap." It was all in pieces. And it would "only cost a little bit to buy the necessary parts to put it together again." This was supposed to make it a real bargain. His wife didn't want it to appear as though she didn't want him to enjoy life, so, against her better judgment, she agreed. Wouldn't it be fantastic though if she were as great a joy to him as a motorcycle?

Sometimes husbands really apply pressure, causing a wife to feel very guilty if she doesn't cater to his whims. Some **two years later**, there was my friend's wife, complaining about that pile of motorcycle parts taking up the same corner of the garage, without ever having been completed. He didn't like those reminders. So, now, his excuse for not completing this task (which was supposed to have been necessary for his happiness) became, "It will cost too much to fix it up." The very reason he gave for buying it in the first place (cost) was now the reason why he felt he should be excused from his obligation to follow through and complete this money-saving opportunity.

Do you think he was alert to his preferential treatment of himself? He wasn't. But he is now. He's learning to see his wife as a blessing from God, helping him to see changes in attitudes and actions that are necessary in his life. He's learning to see with his eyes, listen with his ears, and to be a man of his word, reasoning things out before making decisions, letting his wife be a part, without pressure, of his decisions.

BLIND AND DEAF TO HYPOCRISY?

There are many men who pray noble prayers in church, admonishing wrong, pleading Christ's causes, and that's good. But all the while, sitting next to these powerfully praying men, is a wife who is broken hearted. Not only because of his treatment of her, but because she hears his prayers too and wonders how he can talk so clearly about what needs to be done to follow Christ and still not practice what he is preaching. She wonders whether or not he realizes how hypocritical he appears in her eyes.

Dare she challenge him though?

Ralph, for example, prays at church functions that more people will realize their responsibility to the reputation of Christ by following through with their commitments to the church. Then, when his wife reminds him to prepare his reports for the missionary committee's meeting he chews her out for "nagging" him. No, he didn't have it ready on time even though she reminded him many times.

It seems there are many wives who wish their husbands wouldn't wait until the last minute to meet their commitments. They hear from others too about their husband's failures and it's embarrassing to them. They don't want others to have bad things to say about their husbands. They want their husbands to be respected.

Let's illustrate further, using a car: The proof of a man's desire to understand is in his response to being taught. If he says he wants to understand more about being a responsible car owner, he should discover more about car maintenance. He should welcome instructions and criticisms. If he gets angry when it is pointed out to him that his car needs tires and needs the oil and oil filter changed and that it needs to be washed and waxed as well, one might well question his seriousness about his desire to be responsible. Likewise, if he says he wants to be a spiritual leader in his home, and yet becomes angry as he is shown what he can do that will allow others to see Christ in him, it's likely that his sincerity will be questioned.

BLIND AND DEAF TO SHIFTING THEIR RESPONSIBILITIES?

Willie and his wife Dee had both been putting many many hours into the new business he had begun. After a couple of years it had grown to the point that they either needed to hire an employee, or to purchase additional equipment or to double his time at work to "get them over the hump." The very job they were **then** working on could finance hiring an employee or buying the necessary equipment, but not before the job was finished. So the decision was made to work extra hours.

Wanting to help Willie avoid a common trap that husbands get caught in, I shared this caution with him: It is easy for a wife to see and understand that a growing business will require an abnormal amount of hours in order to bring it to the point where it will serve the family rather than making the family serve it. A wife can see, too, when a business is increasing to the point that additional help is needed. She can also realize that finances won't allow for it yet.

So it's not hard for her to realize that her husband will have to put in additional time in order to get past the financial hardship of adding someone to the payroll or of buying more equipment. So she is willing for him to do whatever is necessary to get past the problem. But if he continues to maintain the extra hours as his "normal work pattern" **after** he is past the problem, she will regret having made the sacrifice to see him get ahead. Getting ahead, after all, was supposed to benefit them both. As it often turns out, though, he is pleased, but she is very unhappy. A common phrase made by many wives is, "His job is the 'other woman' in our marriage."

Having explained all this to Willie, I exhorted him to be very watchful to avoid this type of situation in his business and marriage. Because his wife was standing there with us, she heard the complete illustration, too. Willie, very willing to take steps to make his marriage successful, said something to his wife with very good intentions that put a very heavy burden on **her** shoulders. He simply said, "If you see me starting to give this business greater priority than our marriage, **you be sure** to let me know."

I said to him, "Willie, it's good that you're willing to try to avoid falling into the trap that we just mentioned, but I wonder if you know what you just did to your wife?"

He looked at me with a questioning look on his face that went along with his words, "No, what did I do?"

He did exactly what many other men do in situations like this when they want to avoid a problem. I said, "You just made **your wife responsible** for your success or failure. You just said, in essence. I'm turning this responsibility over to you, and now if you don't let me know when I'm starting to do the wrong thing, it will be your fault."

He responded by saying, "I did?!" while looking first at me, then at his wife, then back to me with a genuine look of concern on his face. His wife said, "He does that to me a lot of times."

To help him realize how being alert to potential problems in his marriage should be his responsibility, I shared the following illustration with him: "There are probably thousands of electrical signals being broadcast into the air at any given moment: radio, C.B., television, telephone, etc. The only thing that keeps you from knowing what they are is whether or not you are tuned in to them. Just so, there are many things taking place concerning a marriage that are signals, and it is your responsibility as the leader of your home to be tuned in to what is going on around you. You must be cautious of those things that will damage your marriage".

"Be thou diligent to know the state of thy flock, and look well to thy herds." (Proverbs 27:23)

Men don't have to be reminded when hunting season opens. Nor do men have to be reminded of the time and date of the World Series and other similar occasions. Why? Because those occasions are very important to them.

This fact proves at least two things:

1. That men can remember details.
2. Many things which can determine the success or failure of a marriage evidently are really not important to men, or they'd remember them, since they can remember things that are important to them.

Another area where men shift their responsibilities is shown in things such as a husband asking a wife to take care of business matters for him. A husband might ask a wife, for example, to order materials for him and then get upset with her for not completing that task. But often a wife fears being asked unusual questions that she doesn't feel confident to answer even though the questions may seem simple to her husband.

Does he show gratefulness for her caution? Too many times the answer is NO. If a supplier were to ask her a question that she can't answer, she fears making a mistake which could cause her husband additional problems. Though she lets him know ahead of time that she feels inadequate to do this for him, he ignores her fear of not being able to handle this task and instead of being gentle-hearted toward her, he makes her feel guilty for not being obedient.

Another frequent area of shifting responsibility is asking a wife to call back an angry bill collector to tell him "what's what." He asks **her** to do this even though **he** was late paying the bill after she warned him many times that it was coming due. But he forgot.

These types of situations cause a wife to feel a huge amount of pressure. It is the job of a husband to find ways to relieve his wife of pressure. *"giving honor unto the wife, as unto the weaker vessel" (I Peter 3:7).* Seeing her husband protect her from unnecessary pressures makes a wife feel that she is cared for.

I remember the time my wife bought an item which didn't prove to be a good purchase. She wanted to return it, but was too embarrassed to do so herself, so she asked me to take it back for her. She was very grateful when she learned that I was willing to do that for her. She had more than just the need for me to return the item for her. She also had the need to feel certain that I was really glad to do this for her. I want my wife to know that she never needs to feel bad or guilty for asking me to help her when she feels pressured. I believe that honoring her as a weaker vessel means not just to recognize my wife's responsibilities and limitations and to protect her from only that which will be **destructive** to her, but to also **lighten her burden.**

Recognizing a grocery bag as a weaker vessel than a cardboard box, you limit the load you place in the paper bag. You don't put 200 pounds of groceries in the bag or it will break, causing damage not only to the bag, but also to that which it was supposed to carry. You don't expect the bag to watch out for itself. The bag is willing to just keep on receiving until it is destroyed. Wives are the same way. They find rejection so threatening, and the need to not fail so strong, that they will continue to accept responsibilities **we** have neglected (or not accepted) until they break down too. Their breakdown might be emotional or physical or they may simply lose respect for us or even become very independent. When a woman becomes extremely independent she is often called, "unsubmissive" or "strong willed," or "a woman who takes matters into her own hands," because she is seen handling more and more of her husband's responsibilities.

Imagine the damage to the spirit of a wife who has spent several years working to put her husband through seminary only to discover that while he was there, he was taught a set of priorities that would almost exclude his wife. He has been given the freedom to feel that he can place church members, the "community to be won", and often even the church building and its care above her in importance. However, I Timothy 5:8 says, *"If any provide not for his own, and especially for those of his own house, he hath denied the faith, and is worse than an infidel."*

We must realize that "provision" involves more than just money. It also includes spiritual leadership, emotional care, as well as understanding, comfort, compassion and friendship. Does this not mean that a wife **must** have very high priority in her husband's life? It surely does!

The "using" of wives by husbands is not isolated only to seminary students. There are many wives putting their husbands through secular college as a type of investment in the family's future.

Yet after all those years of pressure and sacrifice, the wife discovers her feelings and wishes about family plans and goals carry little if any weight now that he sets out in life as a graduate.

Let's look at this type of investment in the future from a business viewpoint. If a businessman told me he would finance me as I trained for a profession, it would be easy to assume that he would feel he were making an investment in me. As such, I should **not** be surprised if he **expected** to have some ''say-so'' about what I did that affected my professional standing. I should also **expect** that he would demand a high degree of respect be shown toward him. **We** probably would have discussed **everything** concerning our agreement **before** he would have entered into it. I'm also sure that I would have had to take the necessary time to clarify **all my thinking** to **him**. It would have been foolish to even think of forcing him to do it my way. Then again if **I** were **in his shoes** and saw that he were doing something **not** in the best interests of **both** of us, and he were to argue with me about it, I would probably withdraw my support immediately!

And yet, while a man is preparing himself for ''the family's'' future, his wife may well be expected to support him **quietly** . . . without freedom to comment, discuss, question or even to know his plans, let alone be an actual part of them.

If we wish to be admired and respected as wise, understanding leaders, we should follow the example of one of the wisest men who ever lived: Solomon. He did not think himself above being questioned about his ways.

''And when the queen of Sheba heard of the fame of
Solomon concerning the name of the Lord, She came to
prove him with hard questions . . . and Solomon told her
all her questions: there was not anything hid from the
King which he told her not.'' (I Kings 10:1-3)

His willingness to submit himself, even as the King, to her questioning caused him to be respected. But even more important, it caused her to worship the Lord God (vs. 9).

It is, however, more common among men to feel it unnecessary to answer the questions of **any** woman, even of their wives. Sometimes that could be written, ''let alone of their wives''. Sadly enough the attitude of not being answerable even to a wife is very noticeable in too many Christian marriages today. Too many husbands manifest the natural inclination to think of themselves as the boss or ruler of their marriage. This attitude is reinforced by the popular notion that a woman's **only duties** in a marriage are to be a silent, obedient, submissive wife. And that submission, regardless of the conditions, better be with a gracious pleasantness or she's not a good Christian woman. Again, there is a focus which expects wives to be flawless while husbands are not.

As you may have noticed, this is one of the longest chapters in this book. That's because another whole book could be written listing example after example of how we need to re-evaluate the injustices of our ways as husbands. In order to be fair, we need to see ourselves through the eyes of the ladies God has placed in our life.

I think it would be important to finish this chapter by saying that if we continue to be selfish in our daily lives by trying to stack the marriage deck in our favor, by ignoring the needs of our wives, **we will pay the price**.

> *"He that troubleth his own house shall inherit the wind . . ." (Proverbs 11:29).*

> *"For they have sown the wind, and they shall reap the whirlwind . . . (Hosea 8:7).*

Looking at Malachi 2:14-15, we find the prophet Malachi has been talking to the men of Israel about the problems they have been experiencing. He's saying that those problems are due to God withdrawing Himself from them. God is allowing them to suffer for their ways. Because of the apparent blindness to their wrong doings, as is often the case with men (as has been pointed out) they must have asked the question, "What did we do that is so bad?" To which Malachi responds,

> *"Yet ye say, **wherefore?** Because the Lord has been witness between thee and the wife of thy youth, against whom **thou hast dealt treacherously**; yet is she thy companion and the wife of thy covenant. And did he not make you one? . . . Therefore **take heed to your spirit**, and let none deal treacherously against the wife of his youth."*

No woman will allow herself to be continuously set up for spiritual, emotional or physical defeat and do nothing about it. The staggering climb in the divorce rate is proof of that. But surely we know that divorce is not the answer to marriage problems.

CHAPTER EIGHT

GETTING OUR
HEARTS TOGETHER

> Does God allow a husband the freedom to disregard his obligation to be a righteous leader simply because he says, "We don't understand one another."?

Would giving your wife the freedom to express exactly how she feels about you and what you're doing cause you to feel threatened?

I was surprised to find that some men are even threatened by the amount of freedom I give **my own** wife. I discovered, too, how threatened many men are when they find that I am teaching other husbands the value of **giving** their wives the freedom to help them see where they need to improve. How threatened are some when they learn that we let our wives be involved in almost all the decision making! "You can't give a woman that kind of freedom!" is the outcry of some men. "She will abuse it!" is the warning.

Why is it that that kind of freedom and involvement seems to frighten so many men? I think it's because it is often seen as a threat to the jealously guarded role of Boss, Authority, or Leader that men **claim** for themselves. No one, however, can claim that role. It must be earned even if a person **has the title**. He cannot demand that others view him as leader. People may, in fact, fear a leader because of his power, and still not respect him as leader.

It needs to be emphasized that we are not suggesting that a wife **demand** the right to express concerns to her husband about his direction and character, but rather that her husband **ask** her to help him see himself through her eyes and to help him think things through from another perspective. As we've already illustrated, it is very easy for men to overlook their own imperfections even though they may be quick to point out someone else's imperfections. Many times, even as a man is pointing out another's needs, those who are listening are aware of that man having identical problems in his life. They even wonder how a man can recognize a problem in others and not recognize it in his own life.

*"Therefore thou art inexcusable, O man, whosoever thou art that judgest; for wherein thou judgest another, thou condemnest thyself; for thou **that judgest doest the same things**." (Romans 2:1)*

Almost no one wants to have his life closely examined. How many times have we heard people trying to escape the pressure of being shown their imperfections by saying "No one's perfect." That should never be an excuse, but a challenge!

REASONING TOGETHER

A wife has a vested interest in her husband's success and reputation; she is building her life around him. Aside from himself she is the one who has the most to gain or lose if he stands or falls. One of the most important things in her life is her husband.

A man who has not made it a part of his marriage to reason together with his wife in as many situations as possible will be setting himself up for difficulty in his marriage.

Most women have a fantastic capacity for being able to think ahead in marriage and home-related situations. Often, in thinking things through, a wife will actually **imagine** what might happen in a given situation, then come to conclusions about what should be done to handle the situation. A man who does not regularly and frequently talk things over with his wife and let her freely talk things over with him will probably find that she hasn't developed a pattern of **waiting** until **after** she has talked with him, to draw conclusions. Then, since she has, without the value of his thinking, made a determination, she will likely take her decision to him in the form of a request. Faced with either accepting or rejecting her request, and not necessarily having the benefit of the thinking that led to her request, her husband is often bewildered to find himself in the midst of a disagreement, or worse, a fight.

ELIMINATING FIGHTS

So many people are unnecessarily arguing over things that don't need to be argued about because they don't think about what is **behind** the argument. Not enough people search out a matter. For instance, let's say that a man's name is BILL JONES and he lives at 712 OCEAN STREET and he's been living there so long that the postman knows him well enough that if he saw him at the local grocery store, he would recognize him and say with a smile on his face. "HI BILL!" Let's say, too, that one day he delivers a letter that is addressed to **JOE SMITH**, 712 OCEAN STREET. So Bill stops him and says, "Hey you delivered this letter wrongly!" And the postman says, "No, I didn't."

Of course Bill insists that he did, because he is not JOE SMITH. But the postman continues to insist that he didn't, because the address is 712 OCEAN. Bill continues, "But you know that I'm not JOE SMITH. Why do you deliver his mail to me? You've delivered it wrongly."

This could go on all day and the right solution would not be reached because both are arguing over the **wrong problem**. The problem is that the person who sent the letter put the wrong address and name together. If the sender will change the name he has with the address, then the problem can be solved.

Let's look at another situation:

Harry had been trying to convince me that Millie was trying to bankrupt him with her spending habits (many men mistakenly think this of their wives). I had been trying to help him see how critical, condemning and harmful that kind of thinking is to a marriage. One day while I was sitting in his office Millie called Harry. I couldn't tell for sure what the conversation was about, but it was a very short conversation in which Harry became very upset and finished by saying, "I'll call you back and let you know!"

Harry then turned to me and said, "Okay, here's a perfect example of what I've been trying to tell you. She **is** trying to bankrupt me. That was Millie and she wanted to know if she could go down and buy a new set of wrought iron patio furniture. I don't understand how she can even ask that question. She knows we don't have the money for that. You said I should learn to listen to her, so what am I supposed to tell her now, Yes or No!?"

He misunderstood the phrase "listen to her". He thought listen to her meant, "**do** as she says."

I said, "Listen to her means, 'Stop placing little or no value on her words.' Concentrate on what she's saying. Learn to hear what her feelings are saying; not only what her mouth is saying. There are more solutions available to you in this situation than just a Yes or No answer."

He replied, "Well, you'll have to show me." He was so emotionally caught up in his prejudice toward her he wasn't free to think of any other solution. I explained that if he could know what his wife were thinking, he would be able to avoid misunderstandings that can cause fights. If he focused on trying to understand her, it would give him the freedom to discover solutions.

Trying to show him the proof of that, I said, "I think I know what is going through Millie's mind. I think I know what makes her feel she needs to buy that furniture. You want to hear it?"

Although he sounded skeptical he said, "Yeah." I felt as if he were also saying, "You think you know her better than I do?" So I started explaining, "We've been meeting with the couples in this workshop at your house since Monday; right? And, we will be meeting the rest of this week including Friday from one o'clock until six o'clock, won't we?"

"Umm Hmmm," he agreed.

"So," I continued, "I think Millie, being the excellent hostess that she is, is thinking ahead: After meeting all day Friday, we're going to have a pot-luck-dinner. The weather has been beautiful. So, she thinks, 'wouldn't it be nice if our guests could have a nice place outside to enjoy their dinner.'"

He listened while I went through the explanation, then questioned, "You really think that's what she's thinking?"

Feeling confident, I said, "I sure do."

He took a deep breath, held it for a second then breathed heavily through his nose. Then he said impatiently, "Okay, so what now. Am I supposed to buy it or not?"

He still wasn't quite with me, yet. He needed to think it through even further. So I asked him, "If I've correctly figured out what Millie is thinking, then how long will she need that furniture?" When he answered, "I suppose just one day," I felt as if he were saying, "Okay, I'll play your little game."

"Okay, since it's not practical to buy patio furniture for just one day, are there other ways to work this out?" I questioned.

"What? rent it?" he challenged.

Wanting him to continue to think this through I asked, "Do you know of anyone who has patio furniture that's not being used?" His eyes lit up now as he started joining in on the search for a suitable solution.

"Y-E-A-H," he said slowly, as I watched his mind visualizing an answer that could make everyone happy. "I have a good friend who owns a motel and he has all kinds of patio furniture. Shall I call Millie and tell her?"

Now he was involved. But he needed to realize more about solving problems. Wanting him to look further down the road, I asked him, "If you call her right now what will be her first thought?" He looked at me with a questioning expression, so I asked, "Won't she want to know if it is available for her to use? Let's first get your plan together so you will have a legitimate solution to present her. Can you call your friend and see if your solution is possible?"

When he called, he found his friend was in the middle of moving and had a beautiful set of wrought iron patio furniture that Harry could use. In fact, his friend asked if Harry could keep the furniture at his house until he completed his move, and then return it to him at his new home. Of course, Harry was getting more and more enthusiastic about this. **Now** he was ready to call Millie back.

As he called her I could still hear the, "Ya-wanna fight attitude," in his voice. So far he was basing his solution on the idea that I **knew** what Millie was thinking and he still had no assurance that I was right. When he told her what he had to offer, she was delighted. As he talked to her, I could hear his attitude changing. His voice became calm and friendly. When he hung up the phone, he turned to me and said, "I can't believe this. Just fifteen minutes ago I was boiling mad at my wife and here I am now all over it and even feeling good toward her."

I concluded, "It's because you took the time to discover what was going on and to meet the need."

He said, "What I can't get over is how you knew what Millie was thinking". I replied, "I learned to discover how women can think by learning how my wife thinks. You can do the same thing too." He is doing the same thing now. Isn't it great to see God prove to us the value of doing things His way, giving us even greater confidence as we learn to understand the mind of a woman by laying down our lives for our wives!

Recently I heard a husband and wife who knew them and who knew how bad their marriage had been say of Harry and Millie, "It's one thing to see an individual man or woman who has peace, but it's really something to see a couple who has genuine peace in their marriage especially since we know how close you two were to a divorce in the past." These friends then added, "Even though we have been considered a normal, happy Christian couple by others, we see that we need and want what you have." Isn't that what Christ meant when He said, *"Let your light so shine before men that they may see your good works, and glorify your Father which is in heaven"* (Matthew 5:16).

The problem in that situation was solved through understanding. Understanding only comes from an investment of time, and a

willingness to discover **where** there is a lack of understanding. A desire for understanding has to be sufficiently demonstrated by the husband, causing a wife to trust that she can share her heart with him and that it **is safe** to do so. In other words, she sees that he wants to learn how to care about her as much as he cares about himself. *"Let every one of you in particular so love his wife even as himself"* (Ephesians 5:33a).

Remember it isn't the problem that's the real problem; it's not knowing how to solve the problem. That's what wears men out.

WHY DOES MY WIFE ASK SO MANY QUESTIONS?

I was sitting in the office of a friend of mine when something happened that changed his attitude about his wife asking so many questions. In fact what he learned helped him to love her even more.

As you may recall, I mentioned that we have a discipleship ministry. One of the special opportunities of such a ministry is that husbands let me help them see their marriages and events surrounding their marriages through the eyes of their wives. It is because these husbands give me this privilege that lessons like the following are learned:

The phone on my friend's desk rang. When he answered it, I quickly became aware by the things he was saying that it was his wife. I figured out how the conversation went by what he was saying. Now that I've confessed to listening in on someone else's conversation, let me tell what took place:

He: "No I'm not alone."

I assumed, she asked, "Are you alone?"

I then assumed she asked, "Who's with you?" because he said, "It's Ken!"

Next, I assumed she asked, "What are you doing?" because he answered, "We're just talking."

What would be more natural than to assume she said next, "What are you talking about?" since I heard him impatiently reply, "Nothing in particular!"

The conversation didn't last much longer and when he hung up, his comment to me was, "Boy, that's one thing that really makes me mad. She drives me crazy with her questions."

"Would you like to know why she asks so many questions," I asked him.

With great enthusiasm he said, "I sure would!"

Trying to prepare him for what he was about to hear, I told him that there is **something** that almost every woman does naturally while very few men do it at all. But, because women think that men think like women do, women are puzzled when they learn that many men do not do this. This **something** that women do takes place particularly while they are asking questions.

Maybe a good way to explain this would be to use this illustration. Let's say you are getting ready to go somewhere and your wife notices it and asks you, "Are you going somewhere?"

Just hearing those words sends up a red flag of irritation to a lot of men because they think their wives are checking up on them. They think they're big boys now and don't need to "report in." Some men just don't remember, or it doesn't occur to them, to consider their wives, considering that they will feel more comfortable knowing if, and where, their husbands are going. So in a way that makes his wife feel guilty for asking because his attitude says something along this line. "Of course I'm going somewhere, is that okay with you, mommy!?"

He may not say those exact words, but he lets her know that he is bothered by her asking questions.

And, even though he has already shown her his resentment, she hesitatingly says, "Where are you going?"

With increased resentment, he says, "To K-Mart!"

Now I realize that because of the resentment evident in their husbands' replies, most wives will stop asking questions at this point. But in order to make a point, I'm going to press this illustration. We'll make this wife a **very brave** woman who keeps on with her questions.

"What are you going to K-Mart for?" she asks with a slight wince.

"To buy some tires!!" he snaps back without cause.

As unfortunate as it is for her to have to do so, she says with hesitation in her heart and voice, "What are you going to buy tires for?"

"For the truck!!!" He's angry now!

Now, in some cases it's getting almost dangerous (especially emotionally) for her so, almost cowering inside, her voice shaking, she asks, "What kind of tires are you going to buy?"

"For crying out loud, white-walls! Will you get off of my back!!!"
he yells back at her.

Just what is it within a woman that would cause her to want to
ask questions and then feel terribly hurt because she thinks **she** is
wrong because her husband is getting resentful about her questions. **She** feels guilty for **his** poor reaction.

Why do questions seem to be so much a part of being a wife?
Here's why. When I use this illustration in a workshop, as soon as I
say, "K-Mart," practically every woman there gets an image in her
mind of the K-Mart she is familiar with. You see, most women
visualize things concerning relationships. Most men don't. Here's
what is happening: A wife, being pledged to her husband, needs to
feel like she is a part of his life. So her questions are a way for her to
enter into his life. She can, **in her mind**, go with him to K-Mart. Let's
go through it again with the responses in a wife that allows a
husband to see why she asks questions.

Wife's   Q.   "Are you going somewhere?"
Husband's   Ans. "Yes, to K-Mart." (Now she **literally gets a**
                          picture in her mind of K-Mart. Now she has
                          mentally joined him.)
                   Q.   "Why are **we** going to K-Mart?"
                   Ans. "To buy some tires." (Now again, she
                          actually visualizes the tire department.)
                   Q.   "What are **we** buying tires for?" she asks.
                          (Now that they are in the tire department.)
                   Ans. "For the truck." (Now she has **a picture** of
                          his dark green truck in her mind.)
                   Q.   "What kind of tires are **we** buying for the
                          truck?" she turns to him and asks.
                   Ans. "White-walls." ("Oh, isn't the truck pretty with
                          it's new white-walls," she might think as she
                          stands admiring this **picture in her mind**, almost
                          as if it's a reality.)

Now this may seem corny, childish, stupid, or even hard to relate
to for many men, but it actually happens and if a husband is not
willing to let his wife enter into his life in this manner, it will cause
her to feel **personally rejected**.

She will feel very hurt, and on top of that, **guilty**. Why guilty?
Because so many women have been told that a **good** wife doesn't

question her husband; she just trusts him. But that implies that her questions are based upon mistrust. In most cases, however (especially in the case of those who are newly married) when a wife is asking questions it isn't because of mistrust, but because of a desire, a need, a craving, to be identified with her husband, to sense that she and her husband are one. He has accepted her into his **total confidence**. That makes her feel as if she is valuable to him, and that causes her to feel complete.

> Incidentally, if my wife does not trust me, I can get angry, react or even reject her. Or, I can discover what I need to do to merit her trust. I could learn how to develop those characteristics that would allow her to trust me. Which of these two ways would Christ choose?

As far as asking questions is concerned, Jesus said he would not call us servants, but friends. The proof of his friendship was that he would let us know what he was doing. He would include us into his life and build a special relationship with us. (See John 15:15)

Also, don't forget that the thing that caused the Queen of Sheba to worship God was Solomon's willingness to answer all her questions. (See I Kings 10:1-9)

This matter of questioning and visualizing can cause a problem. Women tend to think "I'm a human being, and my husband is a human being. Now since I (a woman) visualize things, all human beings (even men) must visualize things too." (Coincidentally, most men also think that all women think with the same thought process men use.) As time goes on, many a wife is hurt because her husband does not show through conversation that he's interested in her. He doesn't let her ask him conversational questions nor does he ask her conversational questions. If he were to ask **detailed** conversational questions, it would prove to her that he's interested in the details of her everyday life. It's hard for many men to even relate to the idea that if a man asks his wife questions, it shows her that he cares.

The husband involved in this next illustration experienced a major breakthrough in his marriage because of a situation involving questions.

The phone rang and on the other end was a wife at the end of her emotional rope. She was distressed by what had just happened. "I need some help. I don't know if I can go on like this."

"We just had a big fight and Dan said to me, 'I don't love you.'"

"Maybe I should come over so we can talk about it?" I suggested. About a half hour later we were in the middle of getting all the facts together.

She had said to him, "I've got to go to the doctor today," and he had responded with his usual indifference, "So go." It was like a slap in the face to her. As she left, his words of indifference were echoing in her ears.

Upon returning, she walked up to him. He was in the garage polishing his motorcycle. Unrealistically, she hoped he would show that he cared by asking her some questions such as, "What did the doctor have to say?", so she stood there for a few moments. But no caring words came from him. Her **damaged** feelings, already damaged by his earlier indifference, were once again wounded. Becoming hurt and angry she went on into the house. But then, remembering that as a member of one of our groups she had a responsibility to be his helpmeet, to remind him to look at his ways and to remind him that he had made a commitment to God to change, she decided to go back out and let him have another chance to respond with Christ-like, genuine, husbandly interest. It would have meant so much to her spiritually, emotionally and even physically. Upon returning to the garage, she stood by him for a moment. Still, he did not respond. (He didn't show her the **inquiring interest** she knew **she would be glad** to show him if he were looking for it. But their marriage was full of situations in which he didn't know how to make her feel loved.) So again, trying to ignore her hurt and trying to sound cheerful, she said, almost in a musical tone, "I'm home." His response, believe it or not was, "Maybe you think I'm blind."

He was irritated by all these bothersome interruptions. It was interfering with his motorcycle getting polished. She lost control. She blew up! "I don't think you love me!" "I don't think you've ever loved me!" Much more along this line was said as well.

Although he was irritated, his next response was the result of genuinely thinking it through. "I think you're right. I don't think I do love you!"

She didn't think about how he was honestly facing himself. She only heard his words and, of course, she was devastated.

I said to her, "I know that what I'm about to say could sound very cruel to you, but this is something I've been waiting two years to hear him say. You see he didn't know that he didn't love you. But now that he can **see** that he doesn't love you, he can also **see** that he doesn't know **how** to make you feel loved. That's the first step toward solving the problem...recognizing that there is, in fact, a problem. If a man insists that he does love his wife even though **he** makes her feel unloved, then it's not very likely that he will think that he has a problem."

This husband's next statement was fantastic. "So what do I do now!" He didn't realize that just that question in itself was encouraging to her.

Wanting to encourage him, I said, "Just the fact that you are asking that question is encouraging to your wife. It shows that you do care to learn."

Surprised, he said, "You're kidding. Just asking a question shows her that I care?"

He didn't know how to experience the feelings of others, not even of his own wife. He wasn't trying to hurt her. No one had ever taught him how to feel for others. He didn't know how to enter into the life of others by inquiring and listening. It has been so rewarding to watch as the Lord had been building in him the ability to understand, showing him how to love his wife, teaching him to welcome her questions and how to picture in his mind, things that will make him able to "live" with his wife in an understanding way.

Now, back to the office where I was sitting with my friend. After explaining all this to help him understand why women ask their husbands so many questions, he said, "Do most women really visualize like that?" At each workshop when I go through this illustration, the husbands usually turn to their wives and ask that same question. Wives, in turn, ask their husbands, "You mean, you men really don't visualize like that?"

Visualizing is one of the reasons, too, that women are frightened by the driving habits of so many men. They can visualize the results of wrecklessness. It's also why they are so alarmed for instance when their small children are out of sight at a picnic or camp-out.

There are dozens more illustrations I could use of wives asking a lot of questions, trying to vicariously enter into their husbands lives through visualization, but I'm sure you have your own illustration you can put in here.

LOOKING AT THE SAME PICTURE?

Have you ever had someone show you a picture like this? This one has two subjects hidden in it. Some people see one, but not the other. Some people don't see either even though they search and search. But when someone shows them the hidden subjects they say, "Of course, there it is! It's as plain as the nose on my face. Isn't that nutty that I couldn't see it before."

In this picture one subject is an old lady in a fur coat, looking downward. The other subject is a young lady looking away and over her right shoulder. The reason it isn't easy to see at first is because it's a confusing picture.

Let's say you saw the old lady and I saw the young lady. Would either of us be wrong because we didn't see the other subject? Of course not! What if I said that you were wrong when you told what you saw and I wouldn't even give you a chance to show me what you did see? Wouldn't you think that I were unfair and narrow minded? Mightn't you think that I were unwilling to learn how you look at things or uninterested in listening? Considering all these things would be a necessary part of building a good relationship with you.

I know husbands who illustrate those exact same attitudes of resistance to their wives, husbands who fail to see other important subjects in the pictures of their **own** lives that wives see and husbands **need** to see. Most men, however, fail to see other subjects simply because they will not listen when it is being explained to them. As we learn to see this particular "other subject" in the picture of our lives, we can use this **new** understanding to avoid problems. We will see more quickly the very reason for most problems and thereby be able to solve them. This understanding will become a powerful tool for building relationships and also a powerful tool for **seeing into the hearts** of others.

Here's an example of seeing into the heart as a means of solving problems: A husband, his wife and I were sitting in my front room. We were meeting to talk about something that had been an irritation to them for a long time. When I asked her to give her side of the story first, she came right to the point, "He is **always** disrespectful and mean to my mother For example, we went over to visit my folks last Sunday after church and the **first** thing he did was give her a **bunch** of bad mouth."

Turning to him. I said, "Do you have anything to say?"

His first comment showed a definite need to be more gentle. "What a liar she is! I don't know how she can sit there and lie like that!"

After he finished telling his side of the story, I said to him, "You're both talking about the same situation but from two different viewpoints." Here's why he felt she was lying.

He said, "She's lying, because when we went over to her folk's house, the **first** thing I did was not bad mouth her mother. When we walked through the door, the **first** thing I did was say "Hi" to her dad. Her dad was sitting on the couch watching the football game, so I went over and sat down with him so I could watch the game too. He and I also talked a little about different things while we were watching. But **later**, when her mother hollered out dinner was ready, we didn't jump up and run over to the dinner table. So she started whining about how she had spent all morning getting dinner ready and how we didn't appreciate it and on and on and on. Finally her dad got tired of all her mother's nagging and went over and punched the TV off. **Then** I said to her mother, 'We should have stayed home, then **we** could have had some peace and quiet. At least we would have been able to see the game without all this hassle.' So the **first** thing I did was not give her mother a **bunch** of bad mouth. And I don't **always** act disrespectful and mean to her."

Imagine the hours of arguing that must have gone on between them before we met because he was arguing over her use of words. However, there definitely were some lessons that would have been good for him to learn in this situation. For example, he definitely needed to learn how to die to himself (give up what he wants for himself, and prefer others first).

But let's not get sidetracked from our goal. What was it that his wife was looking at in this picture of his life? What did she see that he was not seeing?

Because he didn't agree with the way she expressed herself, he insisted she was wrong. But they were clearly talking about the same situation. She was saying **something** different to him though. So what was happening?

They were explaining the same situation for **two** different reasons: she attitudes; he mechanics. Her explanation was focused on and emphasizing his **attitudes**. That's the picture she was looking at. It **wasn't** her goal to explain anything else. (But, since he didn't see what she was looking at, he felt an explanation could **only be right** if she told it as **he saw** it.)

You see, when women talk to us about what we are doing or saying, they usually want us to see the **attitudes** we have. The situation is merely a **vehicle** for them to use while pointing out our attitudes. That's why it's not as important to a wife that the story be told in **exact** order. In her mind the order is not nearly as important as the attitudes. *"A true witness delivereth souls."* *(Proverbs 14:25)* Facing the truth about our wrong attitudes will prosper our souls.

But men, who are usually not watching for attitudes, will emphasize the **mechanics** of something. It's as though they were saying, "If you're going to repeat something, it is only truthful if it is repeated like a movie that has been rewound and then played over again." If a wife rearranges events, then in the eyes of too many husbands, it ceases to be accurate.

Looking at the mechanics only is a very narrow and limiting perspective. It eliminates seeing and understanding an awful lot of what's going on in life. Everyone knows that there can be many different morals to a lot of stories. There are even many truths which can be seen in one section of Scripture.

What I'm saying is this: When women talk about husband and wife relationships, they usually emphasize attitudes and emotions. When a man hears his wife repeating things, he wants (as men put it) just the simple facts! But that's telling a wife what she should or should not see when she looks at her marriage. It's insisting that she see things only from his perspective. But, Scripture points out that it is the husband's responsibility to understand his wife — not vice-versa.

To further understand how men tend to want to accept only the "cold hard facts," see the box on the following page where several examples are listed of the contrasts between what women can see and then what men can see in specific situations.

WOMEN SEE	MEN SEE
A deep violet, soft velvet gown with a delicate lace trim	A dress! (How much does it cost?)
A precious, cuddly, soft, warm little baby that's hungry or wet.	A Kid! (Can't somebody keep that kid quiet?)
A man who makes her nervous when he drives behind her, but will help keep her and her children safe from crime.	A cop! (Who's he after?)
A little old, sweet grandma having a hard time crossing the street.	An old lady! (She's slowing me down)
A romantic dinner at home, dimly lit with candles, followed by sitting beside the fireplace listening to soft music and talking, all alone.	Mush! (I can't see what I'm eating and I'm missing my TV program)
An enjoyable time window shopping together.	A waste of time! (We're not going to buy anything)

Attitudes and emotions are a couple of key items and should not be dismissed. They make life more valuable. It's like the salt and pepper that can make love taste better. A lot of the beauty in life is lost by just looking at the cold, hard facts. The person who refuses to open up to the area of emotions and proper attitudes becomes cold and hardened too.

"But the fruit of the spirit is Love, Joy, Peace, Long-suffering, Gentleness, Goodness, Faith, Meekness, Temperance." (Galatians 5: 22,23)

These are emotions and proper attitudes. It's a wise man who has ears that are listening very attentively for any signs that will show him how to improve. When my wife repeats a situation to me, I could expect her to see it only from my perspective. But it would condemn me to a narrow slice of life if I insisted that I would **only** listen to what I wanted to hear. If I insist that **she see my side**, that doesn't make **me** more understanding. It makes **her** more understanding.

Anyone can **insist** that others understand them. Wouldn't marriages be great, though, if every man would say to himself. "I'm going to demand of myself, that I settle for nothing less than completely understanding my wife even if it seems one-sided. I'm going to insist that she help me see my poor attitudes. I must become more Christ-like." If that is the type of self**less**ness in the heart of a husband, it will not be one-sided! A wife will be drawn to her husband with a deep, deep love for him. I wish that all men could realize the truth of this principle.

And after all, isn't that deep, deep love from our wives what we men have always wanted?

Remember, when you hear your wife explaining an incident, listen. She's probably going to emphasize attitudes. Maybe she will even ignore the order of events, see what attitudes she will reveal in you that are not Christ-like, then get busy; become more Christ-like.

CONVEYING CONVICTIONS

Sometimes, when a husband is expressing his convictions, it will end in a big fight between him and his wife. This will cause him to feel as though his wife is fighting his convictions. But she's usually not. If not, then why are they fighting? (Remember, when there are disagreements, it is a wise husband who asks himself, "Is God revealing poor attitudes in me through my wife?")

The following is an illustration of conveying convictions with poor attitudes.

Steve insists that his family **is** going to church **every** Sunday. However, on Wednesday his mother-in-law became sick and she needed someone to help her out. So his wife Irene volunteered, as any loving daughter might, to pitch in to help care for her mother. This meant that she would have to take care of her home and her Mother's. By Saturday night Irene was exhausted. So she hinted around by saying, "Tomorrow morning sure is going to come around early!"

Steve's response was unsympathetic. "You're **still** going to church tomorrow!"

His response translated to her. "You heathen, trying to neglect God again, huh? It's a good thing you've got me to keep you straightened out." So she said, "I don't have to be in church **every** Sunday to be a **good** Christian, ya' know."

Steve didn't realize that his attitude had been very condemning to Irene. He just felt that his convictions about church attendance were being attacked. So he replied in a very demanding way, "Well, you're going to go to church tomorrow, so you might as well get used to the idea."

Exasperated by Steve's inflexibility, Irene exclaimed, "I'm exhausted, though!"

Still without bending, Steve barked, "That's your tough luck. You have other relatives who could have helped your mom, but you had to be the little do-gooder!" And on and on it went.

Irene was **not** arguing against Steve's convictions about church attendance. Rather, it was his condemning attitude that caused her reaction. What an advantage it would have been if he had already developed the ability to say to himself, "What bad attitudes is the Lord trying to show **me** in **my** life through this situation? Am I being impersonal and putting church attendance above the need in my wife's spirit to feel compassion? Do I make others feel that my rules are more important than my need to love people and to care about their needs?"

A man should be glad his wife cares about her mother, whether she has fifty sisters to help or none. He should also have such a willingness to be helpful that he would also assume part of his wife's duties around the home. Maybe, if possible, he could also go over to his mother-in-law's home and spend some time being a servant to her. Think of how such understanding attitudes could draw many to the Lord. That's the excellent quality he failed to see in his wife: A servant's heart.

I'm thinking of another situation where one middle-aged man's convictions were thrown out like trash because of his attitude. This particular man wanted everyone to be respectful to God. That's not only praiseworthy, it's a commandment. But no one can **demand** that someone else be respectful to God. Wouldn't it be nice, though, if we could cause others to **want** to love and respect God because we represented Him accurately?

With a desire to reach those who need to accept Christ as their personal Savior, several people had rented a building on a main street to use as a meeting place. The public was invited the following weekend to free entertainment and refreshments. The entertainment was excellent. The message was clear. But during the presentations, three young men sitting off to the side toward the back where it was a little darker began to snicker and make comments and noises that were disturbing to many. It was particularly disturbing to this same middle-aged man who happened to be at this event, he said, "as a result of God's calling him, even if it meant leaving his wife and children". They were still living in the Midwest, but he was now on the West coast. He even said he felt God led him especially to this spot to minister to others. When the evening entertainment was finished, most of the people drifted toward the stage or refreshment stand. This left the three young men sitting alone, still making others uncomfortable with their behavior. The middle-aged man could hardly contain his anger toward the three young men. He could hardly wait until the end of the evening when he would be able to go over and talk to them.

The program finished. He got up from his seat, went over to where the young men were sitting and said, "I suppose you guys think you're pretty clever, sitting over there causing all that disturbance." As might be expected they glanced at one another with a smirk. His attack continued. "You think you're pretty smart, don't you? Well, if you keep on the way you're going, you'll end up in hell, which is where you belong if you don't change. Maybe you won't think everything's so funny then." Their apparent indifference to him made him even more angry. Acting as though they were ignoring him, they got up, shuffled around and left.

I'm sure he felt he was serving God by speaking out, and there is certainly nothing wrong with speaking out for God. But the attitude in that man that brought on such an attack can only be expected to bring a poor response in return. Especially if the attack were public! Attitudes are so important. They show what we are. The mouth reveals the attitudes in our heart.

" . . . *for the tree is known by his fruit. O generation of vipers, how can ye, being evil, speak good things? For out of the abundance of the heart the mouth speaketh. A* **good man** *out of the* **good treasure of the heart bringeth forth good things:** *and an* **evil man** *out of the* **evil treasure bringeth forth evil things.** *But I say unto you, that every idle word that men shall speak, they shall give account thereof in the day of judgement.* **For by thy words thou shall be justified,** *and* **by thy words thou shalt be condemned.** *(Matthew 13:33-37).*

Jesus said we must **be** examples of Godly attitudes. They are called "Be" attitudes (Matthew 5:3-12). Additional indication of the importance He placed on attitudes is shown when He said, "You know that the act of adultery is wrong. Well, I'm saying if you look at a woman lustfully, it is the same as committing adultery in your heart and that's just as wrong as the act" (See Matthew 5:27, 28). That means an attitude of lust is the same to God as the act of lust. Dare we overlook then our responsibility to have Godly attitudes? Dare we dismiss others as unimportant (especially our wives) if they say they see improper attitudes in us?

CHAPTER NINE

BEING TESTED

Is it possible to find out how we are measuring up to the challenge of becoming more Christ-like?

Life is full of tests. God has even designed tests for us. That's a method God uses to help us discover our strengths (His ways accomplished in us) and our weaknesses. Scripture is packed with illustrations of God testing and proving men.

Here are just a few:

"And thou shalt remember all the way which the Lord **thy God led thee** *these forty years in the wilderness, to humble thee, and to* **prove** *thee, to know what was in thine heart, whether thou wouldest keep his commandments, or not." (Deuteronomy 8:2)*

"And the **Lord said unto Satan,** *'Hast thou considered my servant Job, that there is none like him in the earth, a perfect and an upright man, one that feareth God, and escheweth evil?' Satan replied, 'What do you expect; you're making life great for him. Take it all away and you'll see he's not so great!' and the Lord said unto Satan, 'behold, all that he has is in thy power.' " (Job 1:8-12)*

"And Jesus being full of the Holy Ghost returned from Jordan, and was **led by the spirit** *into the wilderness, being forty days* **tempted** *of the devil." (Luke 4:1-2)*

"The work of each (one) will become (plainly, openly) known — shown for what it is; for the day (of Christ) will disclose and declare it, because it will be revealed with fire, and the fire will **test** *and* **critically appraise** *the character and worth of the work which any person has done. If the work which any person has built on this Foundation — any product of his efforts whatever — survives (this* **test***), he will get his reward. But if any person's work is burned up (under the* **test***), he will suffer the loss (of it all, losing his reward), though he himself will be saved, but only as (one who has passed) through fire." (I Corinthians 3:13-15 AMP.)*

"But He knows the way that I take (He has concern for it, appreciates and pays attention to it). When **He has tried me,** *I shall come forth as refined gold (pure and luminous). My foot has held fast to His steps, His ways have I kept and not turned aside. I have not gone back from the commandment of His lips; I have esteemed*

*and treasured up the words of His mouth more than my
necessary food." (Job 23:10-12 AMP.)*

*"For You, O God, have **proved** us; You have **tried** us
as silver is tried, refined and purified." (Psalm 66:10
AMP.)*

*"Blessed, happy, to be envied is the man who is
patient under **trial** and stands up under temptation, for
when he has stood the **test** and been approved, he will
receive (the victor's) crown of life which God has prom-
ised to those who love Him." (James 1:12 AMP.)*

I'm sure you can think of many more examples in Scripture of
God proving, purging and building men that He can use.

Testing is a natural part of learning. A test is not bad; it's good.
It is a way of determining our abilities. It is a way of exposing
needs. It's a way of shedding light upon what is or is not valuable.

*"If thou hast run with the footmen and they have
wearied thee, then how canst thou contend with
horses? And if in the land of peace, wherein thou
trustedst, they wearied thee, then how wilt thou do in
the swelling of Jordan?" (Jeremiah 12:5)*

*"If therefore ye have not been faithful in the
unrighteous Mammon, who will commit to your trust
the true riches?" (Luke 16:11)*

We must be proven before we are worthy to serve.

*"Study to show thyself **approved unto God,** a
workman that needeth not to be ashamed, rightly divid-
ing the word of truth." (II Timothy 2:15) "That the **man
of God** may be **perfect, thoroughly furnished unto all**
good works." (II Timothy 3:17)*

Statistics show how that there is a great need for workers in the
field of crumbling marriages. But those workers must be qualified.
Not qualified, however, by men's standards, but by God's standards. The home is a place where a man can learn how to
effectively function as a leader. It is a training ground where
effective ideas and methods are developed; not developed for
other's to use, but for a man's own use within his own family. It is
where a man learns how to discover and prove out God's ways
for his own life. This is where church leadership comes from. (See
I Timothy 3:1-10.) It says, this is a true saying, if a man desires to

serve the church by being a leader, he desires a good thing. A leader must be blameless, the husband of only one wife, vigilant, sober, of good behavior, given to hospitality, qualified to teach; not given to much wine, not a fighter, not after money; but patient, not an arguer, not motivated to want more because he sees what others have; one that rules well his own house having his children in subjection and respectful; (for if a man doesn't know how to rule his own house, how will he know to take care of the church of God?) Not a new, inexperienced Christian, so he doesn't become proud like Satan did. A leader must also enjoy a favorable reputation among gossips, not given to much wine, not trying to get rich; having a conscience that is clear, because of faithfulness to the Savior. First put those who would be **leaders on probation**; then if they are found blameless, let them lead others.

If we go through the trials of learning how to lay down our lives for our wives and experience success, then we become the husbands and leaders God wants us to be. **We** must become victorious soldiers. Then, and only then, do we become qualified to lead others through battles. We must see leadership as "one who is a servant to others." Too often leadership is seen as "one who has others serving him". Learning how to respond with a Christ-like response to the pressure of laying down his life for one's wife and expecting **nothing** in return will prepare a man for the pressures of having no expectations from others as he serves them.

> "And whatsoever ye do, do it heartily, as unto the
> Lord, and not unto men; knowing that of the Lord ye
> shall receive the reward of the inheritance; for ye serve
> the Lord Christ." (Colossians 3:23, 24)

A servant was a **possession** when this was written. He could be bought and sold. He had no rights. Here's how I see this verse: Jesus is the Lord; and I am the servant. So I make the following transfer: I am the servant, and everyone else is Jesus (especially my wife). As a servant, I am willing to make the preferences of others more important than my own. Now I can be happy and excited about doing what is best for others even if I never get to work on my preferences, because it's just as if I'm doing it for Jesus. To avoid sinning as I seek to meet the needs of others, I need to use this guideline: Will doing this cause me to violate God's Word or will it cause me to do anything that is not Christlike? If not, I'm free to serve without reservation. Be careful not to sacrifice your wife and family; making them pay the price for your serving others.

If you discover that it is very difficult to set your own desires and wishes aside in order to become a servant to others, you're normal. Although difficult, not feeling cheated or insecure or even threatened when I don't get my own way can become a normal response. But it is not likely to happen until I come to realize that the world can keep right on going without my opinions or preferences. I don't know about you, but that's hard for me to want to think about and remember. So I need someone to remind me. Maybe I could call that someone my helpmeet.

Here are some tests to think about.

You're going to paint your house. You've visualized it being white with a yellow trim. Your wife would like it to be yellow with a white trim. Since you're doing it as unto Jesus, you do it the way that would please her (for Him).

You're thinking of getting ready for vacation. You've been wanting to go to Disneyland. Your wife has been dreaming of a trip to her mother and father's home in another state. Since you're doing it as unto the Savior you love, you do what would fill her with joy (for Him).

The next test is just as hard.

In each of the above mentioned situations there also needs to be a **sincere joy** in your heart because you realize you have the privilege of being a servant. That possibility is greater if we are concentrating on the following idea: I don't need to have my own way. In fact, in most cases, it really won't make a big difference if I don't get my own way. If a person really thinks of dying to self, he will realize that a dead man is one who does not exist. A man who does not exist doesn't require much to please him, does he? This does not mean a death of personality. It's more like death of the ego.

Asking a man to give up his wants worries some people. They think I'm preaching that a man should give a woman her own way in everything. I'd like to mention this point in defense: Notice that it's only personal preferences or personal opinions, not convictions, that a man is being asked to turn loose. He is not being **commanded** to do it. He is only being asked to **consider** it. This request is being made with the focus of laying down one's life in order to become Christ-like. Here are a few good verses to consider as we think about giving up our wants. Jesus said to God,

"... *Nevertheless* **not** *as* **I** *will but as* **Thou** *wilt."*
(Matthew 26:38)
"Jesus saith unto them, my meat is to **do the will of him** *that sent me." (John 4:34)*

Not what I want, but what you want, God.

After hearing a prophet tell the Apostle Paul that going to Jerusalem would be dangerous, his loving friends pleaded with him not to go. They begged him to be concerned about his own well being. Paul said, *"I'm not only willing to be troubled, but to die for the privilege of presenting Christ."* When they saw that he would not be persuaded to put his own safety first, they said, *"Okay then, the will of the Lord be done." (Acts 21:10-14)*

In each of these scriptures the theme is: be willing to set aside your personal preferences.

There is often the concern, too, that if a wife is shown this kind of preferential treatment all the time, she will develop selfishness.

Might I re-emphasize some Scriptures here. Ephesians 5:25-27 says that if a man will learn how to lay down his life for his wife as Christ laid down His life for the church, then, as Christ, in laying down His life for the church presented the church Holy, so will a man, in laying down his life for his wife, present his wife holy. I'm not making that promise; it's God's promise. If a man has a problem with that idea, then I must ask, "Can we trust God to be faithful to His word or not?" Remember, **regardless** of what my wife is like, I am **commanded** to become an example of Christ to her. Rather than **telling her** to be like Jesus, I need to **show her** how to be like Jesus.

We often think that in order to get what we feel is rightfully ours, we must insist on it, but the Scriptures say just the opposite. To receive (even that which we feel is our fair share), we must give. Your spirit of unselfishness will come back to you. (See Luke 6:38)

Finally, a man who doesn't think that these verses can be safely applied to his wife is demonstrating two things:
1. A lack of trust for God and his word.
2. A lack of understanding about the make-up of a woman.

If you decide to prove God, you will be delighted to discover that a wife cannot resist showering her husband with preferential treatment in response to his unselfishness as Luke 6:38 mentions. Unfortunately, in **too** many cases, a man thinks that **preferential treatment** means **more sex**. But we're talking about the motivation of **unselfishly** giving, not of finding ways to receive more.

On purpose, I am not discussing a man's need to discover the mind of a woman in the area of sexuality. This is, however, an area we do cover in our workshops. Again our goal is to build a **genuine** oneness between a husband and wife. So an aspect of developing that oneness involves husbands learning the **true motivations** and the heartfelt secrets women have concerning sexuality. In the workshops we discuss God's design and pattern for a wife and how many men **expect** women to become the sexual person that **men prefer**, to fit a role designed by men rather than by God.

THE TEST OF KEEPING OUR WIFE ENCOURAGED

Before giving this next test, let me mention a promise from God. A man can choose not to believe God's promise or he can trust that God will do as He says He will. In the Amplified Version Of The Bible, I Corinthians 10:13 says,

"For **no** temptation — **no** trial regarded as enticing to sin (no matter how it comes or where it leads) — has overtaken you and laid hold on you that is not common to man — that is, no temptation or trial has come to you that is beyond human resistance and that is not adjusted and adapted and belonging to human experience, and such as man **can** bear. But God is faithful (to His word and to His compassionate nature) and He (can be trusted) **not to let you be tempted** and **tried** and assayed **beyond your ability and strength of resistance and power to endure,** but with the temptation He will (always) also provide the way out — the means of escape to a landing place — that you may be capable and strong and powerful, patiently to bear up under it."

Now, with this verse in mind, let's carry on. Suppose you come home after a hard day with a lot of pressure and you don't feel that you can handle any more. (Here comes the test: God wants to increase your capacity for handling pressure.) Your wife has had a very difficult day too and needs to unload her burdens on you. At this point you have the opportunity to convey to your wife that **she** can come to you **anytime** with **any** problem and you will minister to her as Christ would.

"Come to Me, all you who labor and are heavy-laden and over-burdened and I will cause you to rest — I will ease and relieve and refresh your souls. (Matthew 11:28 N.I.V.)

Thinking that you've already had enough pressure, you **can** let her know that she **doesn't** have the freedom to give her burdens to you. You **can** let her know that you're upset at her for even considering the idea of giving you more pressures. But you will be failing.

Tests are always designed to prove something. In this case, the test is evidencing the need for Christ-likeness in our responses. In order to prove Himself a worthy leader, Christ went through a great deal more suffering than we ever do, proving Himself a worthy leader and thereby setting an example for us to follow. (Hebrews 4:15, 12:2-4)

If a wife thinks she can't come to her husband because he makes her feel that he will crack or that he can't handle the extra pressure, he will be denying her **one** of the **main** overload outlets God has provided for her. Yes, she can come to God too but if a husband does not allow his wife to use **that** particular outlet God has provided, a spirit of desperation will develop in her.

You may say. "Oh yeah! Well, what happens when I get overloaded?" Don't you remember? God said He would not let you get overloaded. Is He faithful or isn't He?

> I sometimes wonder if God lets my load get heavy as a means of getting me to turn to Him in prayer. Prayer is the means of my getting rid of my desperation.

What kind of desperation would we experience if we couldn't come to our Savior, the One Who is carrying the burdens of the whole world, and dump more burdens on Him. Ephesians 5:25 says we should be for our wife what Christ is for the Church. That's God's design.

What a special privilege to represent Christ to our wife. (Genesis 3:16d). Representing Christ requires that a husband accept the responsibility of protecting and caring for his wife. More marriages need to have an unchanging, genuine, 'til-death-do-us-part' commitment. God has given us a serious charge: to be a husband in the fullest Scriptural sense of the word. If we are disobedient to this charge, we will have to face the consequences. We must not fail to follow the blueprint He has laid out for us concerning marriage.

For example, we men should never feel we have the freedom to excuse our wrong behavior by saying, "God is teaching **my**

wife how to deal with **her** wrong attitudes." Nor do we have the freedom to say, "God is teaching **my wife** patience or trust, because she thinks she is supposed to do the Holy Spirit's job. She doesn't want to wait for the Holy Spirit to speak to me or to wait for Him to show me any of my un-Christ-like characteristics." Nor should anyone else ever try to excuse a husband's sinfulness by encouraging any of these responsibility-passing conclusions.

Certainly a wife has an opportunity to develop a more meaningful relationship with God in these situations, but no one should ever lead her or him to believe that God plans to be tolerant of a husband's sins just to teach his wife to have a proper response. In other words, to imply that the length of time a wife will have to put up with her husband's cruelties depends on how long she takes to straighten herself out, change her naughty ways, respond properly to him; that her husband is God's rod of reproof to her; that he has no control over his un-Christ-like ways; that he's just an innocent pawn in the hands of God; that he's being held back from a more meaningful relationship with God because of her immaturity. This is destructive to their relationship and his accountability and only hinders a man from becoming Christlike.

We can never blame our wives for our failures. We can never rightfully neglect our heavy responsibilities as husbands. It is too serious. Our obligation to represent Christ to our wives is too intensely important to even consider trying to escape it.

All this reading may have revealed some serious needs in your marriage, some deep hurts, some grave wounds to be healed. You may understand now why your wife seems to have withdrawn from the marriage. Maybe you see, too, why she seems to have lost her zest for life or is dead in her response toward you. If so, try to remember that there have probably been times in your life when someone hurt you deeply. Can you remember how you either totally withdrew from them, or how you were very cautious toward them, being very careful about letting them come close to you again? You probably didn't want to give them the chance to hurt you anymore. You may even have avoided any contact with them because you couldn't stand them, and just seeing or hearing them revived the bitterness you felt toward them. If you can remember feeling like that, please let that help you understand how your wife may feel. She may have even said that she has forgiven you. But remember there is a difference between being willing to forgive and feeling free to let someone who has been destroying you back into your innermost self. A wife who has emotionally, and maybe even physically, taken her self out of your life because of severe hurts will be fearful of you, fearing that you will again trample those tender feelings that she has hidden deep within herself. She's protecting herself. She has been trying to become immune to your insensitive ways. Sometimes it takes **years**, before a wife will totally trust her husband again.

DON'T GIVE UP TOO SOON

You've probably seen those TV programs or a movie where the main character has to cross a desert and the whole story is about the struggles he goes through. He runs out of food first; then his horse or truck dies; he gets baked by the sun 'til his lips are cracked and swollen with sores. Just watching, you've gotten exhausted with him 'til you thought you couldn't make it either. Then he runs out of water.

The camera backs away letting you see the whole area around him. As you see him give up, lying down to die, you can see that just over the next sand dune is civilization, with shade, cool water and food.

"Don't give up!," you want to scream out to him. because as a spectator, you can see that he is just about to make the discovery that he's been struggling for. But he does quit, and you feel so disappointed and desperate for him.

I mention that situation because I see so many men give up too soon. A man may struggle for a month or two or even a year or two and then decide that it's time for his wife to recognize the enormous progress (in his own eyes) that he has made. He may even decide that it's time for his wife to stop hurting and see him as a different person now. But the fact that he's ready to quit shows that he is not really a different person yet. Yes, he might be **learning** how to be a different person, but he's not changed enough yet. Only a wife can say when (or if) her husband has successfully made her feel loved.

A man's goal should be: no matter how long it takes, or no matter how much sacrifice I have to make, I'm committed to keep on trying to understand my wife and learn to meet her needs.

I've had times when I felt that I had put out enough effort to prove that I cared. I thought that it was about time I got more honor or relaxation or credit than I have been getting. I started feeling sorry for myself. But I was wrong when I started thinking that way.

I start thinking like that any time I start looking at how much I have improved, at where I have been and where I have come from. Instead, I should be looking at Christ and His example and realize how far I need to go. As time goes on you may find that you're feeling sorry for yourself, too. If so, I can sympathize with you. Still, we must not allow ourselves the freedom to continue in self pity. We must learn to keep on giving of ourselves if we are to receive the benefits that come from giving. *"Give and it shall be given unto you; good measure, pressed down, and shaken together and running over" (Luke 6:38).* We must remember that Jesus asked us to . . . *take up our cross daily and follow him (Luke 9:23).* Our goal, of dying to self should be to become more like Jesus.

It's not unusual to become discouraged. And since we can be faced with it often, whenever we are discouraged, II Corinthians 4:8-12 may be an encouragement. To me it says, "We have many problems everywhere we turn, yet we do not think we are without help. We are puzzled, but we do not think there are no answers; treated mean, but we do not think that no one cares; shamed in front of others for Christ's sake, but our reputation is not ruined in God's eyes. Our suffering allows us to show Christ's response to those who mistreat us. If we did not suffer we would not have the chance to show others what Christ's response would be. Your persecution of us, even unto death gives us the chance to show you, that even though there is death, we have life, through Christ, and you can have life too. We have God's spirit which allows us to visualize, what God intends to do. David said in Psalms 116:10, 'I can say this because I believe it.' So we too can say. 'I wouldn't tell you this if I didn't believe it myself.' "

CERTIFICATES OF LIFE

Although it may seem that the ideas presented here could prove disastrous to a husband, the following testimonies prove what a commitment to the time necessary and a willing heart can produce.

STAFF SUPERVISOR-CHRISTIAN ORGANIZATION

My work involves rebuilding broken lives and relationships. Not only did I attend a great number of Seminars for successful living but I also taught adult education classes on family living. I had been in full-time Christian service for over ten years and thought I had all the answers.

Some circumstances about to take place would soon reveal what I was parroting to others had not made me realize my own needs.

Suddenly, reality came crashing in all around me. Literally overnight I was brought to the realization that I had been consistently abusing personal relationships. I had also totally failed in my marriage. I was more concerned about what others might think of me than I was about what my wife might think of me. Three years ago I realized that I needed to become a "real" person and a loving husband. I also needed to become concerned about inward growth and openness before God. Learning how to become the Christ-like person God wants me to be has been the most challenging and rewarding (as well as hardest) years of my life. I'm learning to trust God and follow his ways in everyday circumstances. I'm finding that God's ways work, even in seemingly impossible situations.

Because of God's grace, I have seen my marriage turn from a disaster and near divorce into a warm loving relationship. I am enjoying a marriage that I never even dreamed was possible.

SCHOOL HEADMASTER

My wife and I attended a week long workshop in April of 1979. My initial reaction to the Biblical principles presented was deep resentment. I resented the focus on me. I have always been quick to see my wife's un-Christ-like attitudes, but have resisted being honest about my own un-Christ-like attitudes. In fact, I could make any of my sins look as though they were her fault.

During that week in April of '79, God stripped me of my defense mechanisms and caused me to see my wife as a helper rather than as an accuser. I know now that God gave her to me to help me to become more like Christ. Because she knows and understands me so well, she is better equipped than anyone else could be to help me see my need to become more sensitive to the leading of the Holy Spirit. God made her that way (Genesis

3:16). Getting to know and understand her (I Peter 3:7) is the most exciting thing that ever happened to me.

God's ways do work! There is now a two-way communication in our marriage that never before seemed possible. The practical advice we received has made this the most wonderful year of our marriage (we have been married fourteen years). Our children are also becoming increasingly more sensitive to the Holy Spirit.

CARPENTER

I have seen the validity of God speaking to a husband through his wife on many occasions. Two of the most memorable times involved the shaping of my career.

The first occurred when my wife felt God speaking to her about having me take over the responsibility of handling the monthly finances, a burden which up to that time I had allowed her to carry. I had always felt that God would indicate the time for her to quit by increasing my salary or providing a job that would equal our combined incomes. She felt that if we were obedient to God's priorities that He would be faithful. So, in a step of faith, she tendered her resignation, even though our financial responsibilities were in great excess of my monthly earnings.

Two days later I was offered a job totaling our combined incomes. My starting day was to be on what was her last day.

This job met our financial needs, but after a time it wore greatly on the family's needs as there was an increasing amount of out-of-town and overtime work required.

My wife, voicing her own need as well as the children's needs of more of my time, suggested that I might possibly seek a career change. I, however, insisted that this **was** the job God intended me to have since He had provided it. As the year went by, things got worse. I finally agreed that if a job offer came with the same salary and a company car (as we had sold our second car) that I would accept it as being God's will.

We began praying. Shortly thereafter I received a job offer that initially looked less attractive but did meet the prerequisites I had stated, so I accepted it. As I discussed the position with my new employer, I stated my priorities of not working nights or weekends as I felt the necessity to spend these times with my family. He agreed to these conditions and has never imposed on me. He even agreed to have family get-togethers when extra job time was needed for conferences.

I am presently employed in the same position, which has not only helped me in meeting the needs of my wife and family but has also become very lucrative in that my boss has generously provided a profit-sharing program too.

Through these and many other instances, I have learned to appreciate the special insights God gives to a wife. I am anxious now to seek out her thoughts and insights on the decisions we have to make and am able to deeply appreciate this additional source of input God has provided, especially since I had previously ignored her for so long.

SHIPPING CLERK

There have been many benefits in becoming a servant to my wife and family. When you really work at becoming a servant you find yourself receiving great joy just from thinking of ways to serve the other person. In the past three years as I've been trying to become a servant to my wife, we have actually become "one" in our marriage. Rarely do we argue now.

SALES REPRESENTATIVE

Our marriage had reached the point where my wife insisted that we get outside help. This surprised me in that I didn't know we were having any serious problems. Through a chain of events, the Lord led us to join with several other couples in this ministry. I had many fears about the method and emphasis of the ministry but decided to give it a chance.

Over the last two years, the Lord has done a remarkable work in the life of our entire family. I have learned about myself and my attitudes by listening to my wife share her feelings. This has been very difficult, even more difficult than I had imagined. However, God has given me a dear gift in my family and He continues to give me encouragement as He brings us all closer to each other and to Himself.

PASTOR

In seeking help for a couple with seemingly insurmountable marital problems, I first encountered the principles leading to spiritual oneness in families. This couple, very special friends of my wife and myself, allowed us the privilege of being present at several of their counseling sessions. As the principles were shared, God began to convict me of deficiencies in my own relationship to my wife and daughter and showed me my responsibility to "love my wife even as Christ loves the church and GAVE Himself for it." This "Christ-like" giving began for me when I finally committed myself to fulfilling several projects dealing with my attitudes toward my wife. These challenges truly accomplished their designed purpose of revealing my insensitivity!

After three years of application, there is still much for me to learn, and I must confess occasional lapses into the old attitudes. However, the joy experienced by working toward spiritual oneness with my wife — as evidenced by her freedom to share her deepest thoughts, desires, and hurts with me — has made every painful step away from self-centeredness worthwhile. An added bonus has been to see these lessons strengthen and deepen my relationship with our nine-year-old daughter. And remarkably enough, as I become more sensitive to my wife's and daughter's spirits, the instances of fruitful ministry with my congregation have increased.

I am grateful to God for the opportunity to learn and apply these life-changing principles. I am also thankful for His continued supply of wisdom and strength to my wife to withstand my periods of rebellion and for her willingness to do it. It isn't an easy way of life, but the results are tremendous — and eternal!

WHY WAIT?

Is your wife still living with you? Why wait until your character forces her to leave before you decide to learn how to live with her in an understanding way. Too many men wait until their wives have left them; **then** they realize that something must be done. This isn't necessary. Why not start learning now? Let her read this book and then give her the freedom to share her heart with you in order that you two can become more and more as one.

☐ I would like to receive additional copies of this book.

☐ I would like to financially support the ministry of
Life Partners, Inc.

Please send me _____ copies of this book at $6.95 each.

I am enclosing $_____ to cover expenses. (Please include $.60 a book for postage and handling).

NAME _____

ADDRESS_____

CITY_____ STATE _____ ZIP_____

Tear Out and Mail To: Ken Nair

3513 E. Onyx Avenue
Phoenix, Arizona   85028